# Frank Sinatra
## The Swinging Narcissist

# FRANK SINATRA
## The Swinging Narcissist

Dr. Harvey A. Kaplan

Copyright © 2017 by Dr. Harvey A. Kaplan

International Psychoanalytic Books (IPBooks),
30-27 33rd Street, #3R
Astoria, NY 11102
Online at: www.IPBooks.net

All rights reserved. No part of this book may be used or reproduced in any manner whatsoever including Internet usage, without written permission of the author.

Interior book design by Maureen Cutajar, gopublished.com

ISBN: 978-0-9985323-9-4

To Katharine, Caroline, and Don

*You only live once, but if you do it right, once is enough.*
—Frank Sinatra

# Table of Contents

| | | |
|---|---|---|
| INTRODUCTION | | 1 |
| CHAPTER ONE | The Legend | 5 |
| CHAPTER TWO | His Personal Calling | 23 |
| CHAPTER THREE | The Productive Narcissist | 43 |
| CHAPTER FOUR | The Ultimate Gamesman | 83 |
| CHAPTER FIVE | His Second Self: The Transformation of Sinatra's Personality Through His Art | 111 |
| CHAPTER SIX | The Man of Action and Conflict | 135 |
| CHAPTER SEVEN | His Legacy | 163 |
| CONCLUSION | | 193 |
| BIBLIOGRAPHY | | 195 |

INTRODUCTION

When I was 12 years old, my aunt took me to see and hear Sinatra doing a live radio broadcast. By this time, his rendition of "I'll Never Smile Again" had filled the airways and enthralled the country. My mother and her friends thought highly of him, and then he caught on with my brother and me, but as adolescents we had other interests, like sports. However, I will never forget the present my uncle brought us – a phonograph that few other apartments had. And from then on we started buying Sinatra's records, mostly to make our mother happy and excited.

When my aunt offered to take me downtown, I was very excited at the idea of being present at a live radio broadcast at hearing Sinatra, so of course I accepted gladly. We caught the train to the studio and took our seats as far up front as we could. And then we waited impatiently. After some minutes, Sinatra entered. He didn't look so heroic to me, rather kind of skinny and bashful. But I had never experienced a radio broadcast in person, so it did hold a great deal of excitement for me.

The orchestra started playing and Sinatra moved toward the microphone and eased into a song. I remember the song until this day: it was "Dream." How can I forget how the words rolled from his lips? And as I listened, I started to feel a chill or quiver running up my spine – there was something in that voice that was so riveting and enthralling. Part of me felt uncomfortable at being so fascinated by that voice; but the other part knew he had a certain power to captivate his audience. And for the next half hour I sat still, totally focused on him.

After the show was over, my aunt led me to the front of the stage and approached Sinatra, while holding my hand very tightly. She stopped in front of him and waited until a few other people were finished talking to him. Then she addressed him.

"Mr. Sinatra, I would like to introduce you to my nephew, who just loves your singing."

He looked down at me with a big grin and said, "Why, thank you," and then shook my hand.

I looked back at him slightly frightened, and replied, "Mr. Sinatra, you're the greatest!"

His grin widened and he thanked us both again and moved on to another group of well-wishers.

As we left, my aunt remarked that what I told him was so nice and asked me if I really meant it. "Oh yes," I exclaimed, "He really is something. I don't think I have ever felt this way about a singer before."

After this encounter, I became a loyal Sinatra fan, and then was able to enlist my brother in this devotion. From that time on, we exchanged mementoes of Sinatra at our respective birthdays. Through the years, I attended many Sinatra performances, always feeling that same initial sensation. I am writing this book to make sense of what his presence has meant to me over the years and to see how I can creatively describe the impact that his life has made in this world. I still feel that he is the greatest, and I also know that he has made my life fuller and richer by his presence. It almost seems as if I have inhabited his world, and have been the happier for it.

## HOWARD COSELL INTRODUCES FRANK SINATRA

On a beautiful Saturday evening, October 12, 1974, together with some friends, I went to see a concert of Sinatra's at Madison Square Garden that was billed as the main event. While we were walking there, we all felt a tinge of excitement, as if the air around us were infused with a special kind of energy. When we got there, we saw that every seat had

## Introduction

been taken, and that the crowd was a bit hyped up with the anticipation of the impending concert. And who but Howard Cosell should introduce Frank? Howard was a favorite of heavyweight fighters and of course of Monday Night Football. And now he was going to introduce another heavyweight, and I thought, *what a fabulously creative idea.* The performance stage resembled a boxing ring, as Cosell entered and the music started to pulsate.

Here is Cosell's introduction at the next night's concert, which was shown on television. His voice had a pompous, strident tone that punctuated every sentence, which only added to the eagerness of the crowd who came to welcome their own champion of song.

"Live from New York—the city of landmarks familiar all over the world, the world center for shipping and transportation, communication, finance and above all entertainment. A city that pulsates always because of the millions of people who live here and work here and visit, and at the heart of the metropolis, a great arena, Madison Square Garden, that has created and housed so many champions. Which is why tonight at the garden the most enduring champion of them all, Frank Sinatra, who comes to the entire Western hemisphere live with The Main Event—Frank Sinatra in concert, Madison Square Garden, October 12, 1974, jam-packed with 20,000 people plus, just people, people from all walks of life, people who are young and people who are old, here to pay homage to a man who has bridged four generations and somehow never found the gap. Hello, this is Howard Cosell and I have been here so many times, this main event carries with it the breathless excitement and anticipation of a heavy weight championship fight . . . but here coming through the same tunnel as so many of the greats, who has the grace and who has the control, who understands the composure and knows what losing means and has made the great comeback. Here he is: Frank Sinatra." (And the crowd went wild.)

One thought I had at that time was:, *who else would have been introduced in this fashion?* Who else had the conceit, and feelings of self-importance to avail himself of this charged presentation? And, of course, I immediately realized that there would be no one else who could have fit into this arrangement, billed as a heavyweight fighter who had weathered all sorts of storms and emerged a winner, who had triumphed over all kinds of adversity and now had emerged as a symbol of success, leaving us with this rich and precious legacy.

Possibly, Sinatra's voice will increasingly come to seem like one of the last things nearly everyone can agree on, that would make people come to an aesthetic consensus all around, in the final flicker of modernity's embers. It is doubtful that any singer will ever again possess this kind of authority. Who could reign as the sovereign of so much territory certainly ever again? Maybe he is our last voice.

What is it about this man that transformed him from what he was-- just a kid with a voice and a dream from an Italian neighborhood in Hoboken, New Jersey—to what he became: the man with the voice, living the American Dream as an international star, and arguably one of the most important cultural figures of the twentieth century. This is a man who has truly lived his life: just about everything he did, he did with passion and desire. This book will try to answer these questions as well as try to make sense of why he is such an important figure in the annals of American culture.

CHAPTER ONE

# The Legend

Frank Sinatra was the greatest vocalist in the history of American music. He elevated popular song to an art and was a dominant figure in the entertainment industry.

Sinatra's music was the embodiment of the popular American song. No pop singer before him sought or achieved so complete an identification, both personal and emotional, with his material. Through him, involvement and intensity became the touchstone of popular singing. Jonathan Schwartz says that when Sinatra took material and ran it through the prism of his instinct, what one heard on record or stage was something so stirring that it was not really possible to speak of any other performer of the music in the same breath or in the same way.

The admiration he drew from a timid press more than compensated for the beating he sometimes took from the public media. No other performer in American show business has had a more controversial public life than Sinatra, nor has any other performer prompted writers to use unabashedly cosmic epithets to describe him. As Pete Hamill says, "Sinatra is loved, he is hated, but it is hard to imagine America over the past five decades without Frank Sinatra as part of its basic fabric." (Hamill, *American Legend*, p. 65)

The impact of Sinatra's persona extends beyond his own concerts, recordings, and casino performances. It extends beyond the army of musicians who have been so lavish in their praise of his musical talents.

And it extends beyond the legions of fans who have adored his singing over the decades. For many, Sinatra has assumed the iconic character of an American cultural institution. He has served not only as a reference point for romantic music and even romance itself, but also as a guide to personal conduct. He is an inspirer of dreams of success. The legendary Sinatra is part of our everyday experience. As he aged, even with his declining powers, which would have demythologized a lesser hero, he continued to receive our unqualified respect. Within the pop-culture psyche, Sinatra was more than an aging man or a superstar or a hero. After more than fifty years of media exposure, he is a legend; and, as is the case with all legendary personae, history is far less important than image.

Sinatra was the first popular performer to exploit the possibilities of this age of mass media, and the myths and images he managed to trade on are the result of a unique confluence of circumstances. His prodigious talent, revolutionary leaps in communication and technology, and shamelessly Dionysian life lived always in the public eye united with a strong middle-class population that had economic influence to exert, and with a culture that came increasingly to prize individuality more than loss of self in community. In his own way, and often on his own terms, he managed to defy the transitory nature of popular culture, becoming the first singer to record continuously for seven decades, staying in the public eye throughout that time.

Sinatra was a human icon whose appeal and powers far transcended his human attributes and talents. The term *icon* itself is derived from the Greek word for "image," Most people "know" celebrities not as they do ordinary human beings, but literally as images: on small screens in their homes and large ones in movie theaters; on millions of mass-produced albums; and in newspapers and magazines distributed all over the world. It was a voice, Bruce Springsteen would later say, filled with "bad attitude, life, beauty, excitement, a nasty sense of freedom, sex, and a sad knowledge of the ways of the world."

The second thing you remember is the attitude: the booze and the broads and brawls, the hat worn at a rakish angle, the jacket flung over one shoulder, the Camels and Jack Daniels, the late nights in Vegas.

## The Legend

> "He was the guy who radiated Bogart's tough-guy cynicism and Fitzgerald's wistful romanticism. He was the hipster and the dreamer, the swinger and the existentialist, the ring-a-ding-ding showman and the melancholy singer of the blues–the first of the great American heartthrobs who made girls swoon and the first big-league avatar of the new celebrity age." (Kakutani, *NY Times*, 5/17/2005)

He overhauled the interpretation of popular song, revising its rhythms and instrumentation, burnishing its lyrics, and establishing the modern code in phrasing. Through his singing, Sinatra was able to evoke an intimate, intense and distinctive experience.

Within Sinatra, there was a hunger for perfection, a driving force to attain an excellence in his singing. He had a root of restlessness and dissatisfaction which exists in all of us, as part of our human spirit. Sinatra was continually on the move, driving himself onward and upward. We need heroic models in whatever areas they may perform, business, war, charity, politics, and, in Sinatra's case, artistry. We need to have heroic models to try to live up to: patterns of excellence so high that human beings live up to them only rarely, even when they strive to do so; and images of perfection so beautiful that living up to them or seeing someone else live up to them produces a kind of "*Ah!*"

Sinatra was not merely an entertainer. His role was far more powerful than that. He exemplified a purport of deep meaning, which was at times even frightening. Once he achieved his superstardom, he did not quite belong to himself. Great passions were invested in him. He was no longer treated as an ordinary human being. His exploits and failures had great power to exult/exalt, or even depress. When people talk of his achievements, it is almost as though they were talking about a secret part of themselves, as if the star had some secret bonding, some Siamese intertwining, with their own psyches.

Sinatra touched something vulnerable in the hearts of so many millions. He seemed to acquire some form of magic, some miraculous power, some beautiful achievement, like the deeds of dreams. He also exemplified the wish in all who grow old that they may retain their powers through the years, against the harsh weathering of time. Some truth about life, some deep vein of ancient emotion and human imagination—this is the chord Frank Sinatra's performances happened to strike.

Part of his glory was simply the result of modern communication, ballyhoo, and publicity. But for those who saw and understood the nature of his gifts, his beauty spoke for itself, his excellence pleased, and something true and universal shone out.

Sinatra, like all great, self-created myths, lives in the excitement of our imagination as a spirit that will not be quieted. He remains a singular figure in this age of mechanical reproduction, because he proved over and over what art can do: destroy, remake and nourish the soul. His music crashes through the wall of indifference with unconquerable sound, as an immeasurable feeling.

His songs include a wide array of emotion, from frustrated love to loneliness and feelings of injury. He became the prototype of all of us, and expressed for us what we have all felt. And the more effective his struggle against it, the greater the universality of his art, and the greater his humanity implicit in the intuitive interpretation of his art. His art was expressed in how he transformed his pleasure and pain, his strivings and dreams, into the continuing expression of his life.

## RELATION TO MARIA CALLAS

There was a way Sinatra's voice was composed and structured so that when he threw a lot of energy into it, the way an athlete does, the coordinations that responded were balanced and efficient. Some critics have cited this phenomenon in the renowned opera singer Maria Callas. The diva more than made up for her vocal flaws with her talent for bringing music to life. Her imperfections set her apart, and her ability to find the emotional meaning in a role was unsurpassed.

One critic made this assessment:

> "One thing about her voice that made it so striking is that it was unlike anyone else's. Sometimes, it had a hollow sound, sometimes a very dark sound, sometimes a little shrill on top. So it was an extremely distinctive voice. More important, I think, was what she did

with the voice; how she used the voice as an expressive instrument."
(Huffington, 2002)

She brought a sense of daring back to opera. She challenged her audience and never bored them.

He goes on:

"The thing about Callas was there was always a keen dramatic intelligence and a real sense of harrowing intensity to her singing, which I think made her extremely special. I mean, when you listen to Callas, even after her voice had started to go, it still tends to be an unforgettable musical experience."

There certainly is an evident similarity between Sinatra and Callas, even though they both sang in entirely different genres.

The lives of talented men and women abound in episodes of inhibition, despair, moodiness, irritability and restlessness that alternate with episodes of productivity and a sense of triumph, confidence, or calmness. We must recognize that artists are endowed with a very high level of sensitivity of perception, both to themselves and to others. They have an inborn capacity to communicate these moods to their audience. The difference then, between artists and other people can only be made manifest by that communication—not by their behavior.

Their dark sides are more understandable seen in that light, and that doesn't necessarily indicate that they are mean, cruel, or lacking in empathy—it means that at times they are subject to a heightened sensitivity or even a feeling of inner torment. Given these varied and deep feelings, an artist such as Sinatra powerfully enables the audience to identify with his characters and point of view, his gestures, or his musical style. When we have an exciting evening in the theatre we embrace the experience, and we identify ourselves with the created characters and react as though we ourselves were alive upon the stage. We feel the lyric, understand the conflicts of love and loneliness. We work up to the self-same pitch of crisis and climax and "let go" only slowly, and then we are able to recover ourselves as audience rather than participants. This is what makes a Sinatra as well as a Callas performance—the element of theatre.

## How is this Effect Achieved?

As Orson Welles once said, "Sinatra doesn't just walk on stage, he plants a flag." Sinatra was able to bring this about in his performances in a number of ways. Aside from certain physical and sexual gestures, physique is but the framed canvas on which the character must be painted. We become completely absorbed in the song and the way it is performed, carried along by his attitude, postural grace, aptness of gesture, stance, and the rhythm of emotion. We refer to this capacity as the "prose and poetry" of the performing body. In addition, there is the quality of his speech—the ability to range from vibrant lyricism to despair and sadness. The audience identifies with his performance, and they almost become him, via his attitude, his voice, his creative interpretation. All of these things erupt and reverberate in waves and echoes standing in dynamic relation to him, and create the situation and give it form.

Fans felt an electrical jolt of excitement when Sinatra walked out on stage—thanks to his image and his personal magnetism. There was a drama to his entrance, and part of the art of his performance was predicated upon his awareness of his audience's expectations and his manipulation of those expectations.

The challenge is for the artist to attract and force his feelings upon the audience, and give them no alternative but to experience his interpretation as it swings through conflict, crisis, climax and resolution. The audience must be drawn in and aroused; the singer's actions must master the portrayal of motion and emotion. To move one's audience is literally that; it cannot be accomplished without the quality of suspense. To be successful, the artist must know the personal elements of human character, the parts of us that respond in kind. These emotional realities make up a force that lies within our unconscious. It is impossible to "see" or to "hear" the unconscious; it is only possible to construe what lies within it. When we say that an idea was unconscious and has now become conscious, we do not mean that it existed in the unconscious in the same form in which it presents itself in reality.

The true creative artist has more at his disposal, special gifts that enable him or her to venture beyond the borders of the unconscious to the mysteries, excitement, pain and joys of life. Artists live closer to their dreams and instill into everyday life a unique kind of magic.

The artist must become aware of those deeper emotions and must transform them into everyday reality, where they can then become discernible to the audience at large. In this vein, Sinatra was an interpretive artist, consistently devoting his life to the exquisite and enduring expression of his own individual reality in the world. Art is essentially a transformation of deeper feelings; the energy bound within the artist must be transformed into reality, and the artist knows how to "find his way back to reality" from the world of private fantasy. In Sinatra's performances, he gives full play to his erotic and ambitious wishes. He finds a way of returning from his world of fantasy back to reality, and with his special gifts he is able to mold his fantasies into a new and more exciting kind of experience.

As a true artist, Sinatra understood how to elaborate his daydreams, and he had special gifts, the mysterious ability to shape his particular material until it expressed the contents of his fantasy faithfully. In this process, energy for transformation is freed—a process which appears to be driven by a heightening of various sexual forces which results in a form which is implicitly interpretive and quite pleasurable to the audience. The way to be an interpretive artist is to know how to give performances the aspect and feel of life, so that people are moved.

## THE ARTIST AT WORK

There certainly exists something we can refer to as a creative thrust, a force that drives creative work. It provides intrinsic pleasure together with the extrinsic courage to go on and face an audience night after night. Sinatra as a consistent artist is driven by a vision of the possibility of newer and greater formal interpretations of feelings that he suffers and by which he is stimulated. He is compelled to execute his art. It is a gift, an inherent endowment of compelling visionary sensitivity, which enables him to transform unconscious inner emotions to conscious outer emotions. In turn, these shape new and greater possibilities of formal interpretation.

This process requires devotion, development and practice in order to realize the artist's intent of fashioning true artistic results. He must wrestle with the forces that make for life and those that pull life toward pain and anguish. The artist pioneers, invents, and truly brings a new idea into music. In short, he or she creates and in this process attains the stature of a legend. He searches for the exact line, the proper balance, color, and rhythm, in order to capture reality in all its subtle interrelationships, and is able to transform his impulses, pleasures and pain, and strivings and dreams into the continuing story of his life. This is the story to which listeners so easily react to and with which they identify. The greater the artist, the more intuitive, the more implicitly interpretive, the more complete will be the emergence of his deeper emotional life. In this process, Sinatra knows what to transform, how much to transform, and in what manner to transform; this almost represents an artistic instinct.

## Transforming the Emotions of His Inner Life

Throughout history, great artists are famous for their frustrated "great loves," which betray the marks of their self-absorption. This experience has played its part in the lives of Beethoven, Goethe, and Brahms. In many artistic types, there is a feeling of profound injury rather than a lack of an ability to love. These great artists struggle against feelings of injury and become the prototype of all of us, expressing what we have all felt. And the more effective their struggles against these feelings, the greater the universality of their art and in turn, the greater their human intuitive and interpretive power.

There certainly are many famous and violent examples of frustrated "great loves" in such fiery men and women. Beethoven, the greatest musical genius of all time, sought by hundreds of women, endured the bitter humiliation of Giuletta's marriage to a young count, a dandy and a dilettante. Beethoven's grief, love, humiliation and rage were forecast in the *Moonlight Sonata*. This piece, written with the frustrated love of Giuletta in mind, shifts the heart's emphasis from the love he cannot have to the love that he has the strength to create. When sometime later Giuletta comes to Beethoven and offers herself, recognizing that she has made a mistake, Beethoven turns his back on her. He renounces the possibility of creative love with her; the forge of frustration has bent his defenses firmly against an old injury. He can no longer enjoy the exquisite possession of what she once meant to him.

Is this not what happens to everyone? Yet when it comes to expressing and feeling this emotion, ringing all its changes, how many other singers could express and interpret it as Sinatra did? Just listen to "I'm a Fool to Want You," sung so deeply with Ava Gardner in mind. He came into the studio and sang the lyric in one take. He then grabbed his coat, slung it over his shoulder and left, totally bereft.

Sinatra would follow his own advice. He felt that he had an inherent capacity to "take in" impressions that needed expression and to transform those impressions and emotions imaginatively in his singing. It certainly was a gift, but, more than that, he was able to give credence to the feelings and convictions we have in our own lives.

What Sinatra chose to interpret and how he did it highlights the essence of his art. What he reveals to us that enriches our pleasure and our understanding is that as a supreme artist he continually perfected his craft. His unique and versatile productivity of high, enduring quality became one of his most important assets. He exhibited such a sense of direction from the time of his adolescence—he knew what he wanted to do, and more than that, he knew what he had to do.

## HIS UNIQUE STYLE

Billy Wilder, the director, described something in Sinatra that is beyond talent: "It's like some sort of magnetism that goes in higher revolutions."

Opera singer Robert Merrill puts it this way:

Singers want to develop a style. They work at it, strive for it, sometimes they contrive it. Sinatra instinctively had a style. I mean, he was born with it. And it grew as he matured. Serious musicians regard him as an artist, a fine artist, a great American interpreter of our music. The beauty of Frank is that he is word-conscious and story-conscious and that's why he's so great. He's a storyteller. He's sensitive—so automatically he's sensitive to his words, to the story they tell. What you are comes out in your music. (quoted in Sinatra, N.,1986)

## Paradoxes of a Life Transformed

There is an extraordinary power infused in this conflicted man, whose tangled and obviously lonely life was a strange mixture of elegance and rudeness, of profound failure and amazing success, of adamant loyalties and equally adamant dislikes, of kindness and courtesies and insolence. These contradictory aspects of his life are what add to the character of a man who was both loved and feared, respected and hated.

After more than fifty years of singing and acting, he had become a legend. He projected a distinctive image: he could be riveting, swinging, dashing, sexy, aggressive, soulful, yearning, and lonely, a fun guy, a sad guy. Someone full of action, someone dangerous, someone loving. He is perhaps one of the most significant figures in all popular culture, Chairman of the Board, The Voice, The Swooner, Ol' Blue Eyes. Whatever the nickname, Frank Sinatra was the great survivor of pop music. Icon of panting 1940's bobbysoxers, Oscar-winning actor in the 1950's, guru of Rat Pack cool in the 1950's, grand old man of pop in the 1980's, Sinatra continued entertaining new legions of fans as the years rolled by. The voice, once as rich as fine red wine – "a sip of sparkling burgundy brew" – faded with the years; as early as the 1950's, it showed signs of strain, the victim of too many boozy, smoke-filled nights.

But it really didn't matter. His ability to vary his tone was what mattered: the saloon songs, served up in all those moody, wee-small hours, Jack Daniels arias of unrequited love: "Set 'em up, Joe. I've got a story that you ought to know..."

The celebrity chronicler Thomas Thomson once summed it up this way: "Is there anybody whose whole voice does for him what his had done for us, all of us?... all of whom recollect Sinatra drifting over from the phonograph in the corner of the living room, the fire low, the wine spent, Sinatra murmuring reassurances. Sinatra, every man's advocate of seduction. Sinatra, every man's ally in romantic defeat."

## MAKING THE WORDS HIS OWN

But with Francis Albert Sinatra, as well as the voice, the words were the thing. Nobody ever treated lyrics the loving way he did. With precise diction that enabled you to hear every word, he made songs his, made them sound as if they'd sprung from his heart. "No pop singer before him sought or achieved so complete an identification, both personal and emotional, with his material," said Sinatra biographer Arnold Shaw (1982). "Through him, involvement and intensity became the touchstone of popular singing."

It's no wonder composers from traditionalist Irving Berlin to modernist Stephen Sondheim preferred his rendition of their tunes. It's no wonder that in 1973, the Songwriters of America named him "Entertainer of the Century."

## SINATRA THE MAN

But apart from his music, Sinatra the man was complex and contradictory, capable of incredible kindness: his acts of philanthropy, big and small, were legendary, together with his blinding rage. Even those who admired his talent were wary of that "other" Frank, the one dubbed the Monster, a man who could and would lash out without warning. As bandleader Tommy Dorsey, Sinatra's early boss and mentor, put it: "He's the most fascinating man in the world, but don't stick your hand in the cage."

Frank was born fighting—the doctor who delivered him thought he was stillborn—but his grandmother never gave up the battle. An outspoken crusader for racial and religious tolerance, the friend of presidents and mobsters alike, Sinatra did whatever he liked, befriended whomever he liked, married whomever he liked, took plenty of flack for it…and went right on doing it.

As he sang in his signature song: "The record shows . . . I took my blows . . . and did it my way."

Once Sinatra stepped onstage or into a recording studio, however, the outrages and outbursts were all but forgotten. All that mattered then, all he cared about, was taking a song on a glorious trip to the moon, singing it for all it was worth. That alone will be Frank's lasting legacy.

"I hope you live to be 400 years old," he once told an audience. "And may the last voice you hear be mine."

Sinatra is loved, he is hated, but it is hard to imagine America in his time without him. He is part of its basic fabric. Part of the reason for his stature has to do with talent, but sheer talent alone has never made icons of performers. How many people who can sing are waiting tables? How many who record albums ought to be waiting tables? There are very good singers, like Jack Jones and Steve Lawrence, who have not become icons even though they have worked steadily at their trades for many years. Part of the reason may be luck or opportunity, but luck is not enough to give one a long run in a fickle business, much less a seven-decade run. The body of material that Sinatra has left behind is truly extraordinary, as is the quality of most of it.

## FASCINATION WITH THE MAN HIMSELF

However, that body of material might well have been forgotten by most people, declared dated and obsolete, were it not for the continuing fascination with the man himself. Through his work and his behavior in the public eye, both of them uniquely American in style and outlook, he tapped into the psyche of a nation, and has mined both the myths that we subscribe to collectively and those that we wish we could live by individually, such as the myth of success.

He carried the baggage of an explosive and passionate life with him onstage, and the songs he sang evoked his own alternately lonely and swinging existence. Every new headline created a new audience. And he kept the celebrity light glowing far longer than any other contemporary figure, thereby keeping his art alive despite changes in musical fashions. Both his prodigious talent and his feisty behavior made him one of the most extraordinary entertainment figures of the century.

By middle age, even with a well-worn voice, every concert was another brick in the building of a legend. This need to work was not so pronounced in other pop stars, such as Como and Crosby, who rarely appeared in concert in their middle years. Their voices remained unblemished and less interesting.

## Seasons of Feelings

Like no other performer, Sinatra has touched this deep feeling of aloneness, with a hint of the irony that feeling alone in the midst of a lonely crowd can bring. All great pop stars sing of love and love lost, but none has dug so deeply as Sinatra.

His songs have all the essentials for the growth and change of discovery, failure, and rebirth which is the core material of art, and resonates with the seasons of anyone's life. The evolution of Sinatra, the bow-tied "crooner," began early. Through the years, he transformed himself from a lead in a vocal group ("The Hoboken Four") to band singer in 1939 with James, and after a rewarding interlude with Tommy Dorsey (1940-42), he emerged as a polished gem of a performer in 1943. He didn't choose just to sing his songs as historical artifacts. Rather, he immersed himself in their emotions and subtly reshaped them and, by the 1950s, had woven them through the loom of his own life and spun them out again as "Sinatra whole cloth."

## The Use of his Body

Seeing Sinatra in person gives one a tingle from feeling the vibrations coming from the stage, because part of Sinatra's great success was that he exuded uncommonly powerful energy from his body. His physical presence and personal authority dominated that of others in the group. When Sinatra appeared on stage, he conveyed all that concentrated power. He was a force, an auditory presence, even in silence. Combine the charisma with his voice, dramatic acting ability, a full orchestra, and some of the greatest songs of the twentieth century, and you are in for a show.

He infiltrated the Western world's dream life. He is "the most imitated, most listened to, most recognized voice of the second half of the twentieth century." (Taraborrelli, 1997) His tape-recorded voice was heard by the Apollo 12 astronauts as they orbited the moon, and his 206 CDs currently in print make him the most comprehensively digitally-preserved music-maker in the history of recorded sound.

In the eyes of the American public, he had reached the status of a legend in his lifetime and beyond. When he came to New York, the only thing Earl Wilson, the popular Broadway gossip columnist, had to write in his column was, "He is here." His readership would know exactly whom he was writing about.

The truth of the matter is that Sinatra poured so much of himself into all his best performances that his version of many songs became the definitive one. Other men and women have composed what he sings, yet his is the final touch which gives their songs completeness, the shapes and colors by which we remember them.

In the words of Sammy Cahn, who with Jule Styne dates back to the early days of "I Fall in Love too Easily" and "What Makes the Sunset"

"I don't sit down to write a Sinatra song. I write a song, then he sings it, and he makes it a Sinatra song."

## STANDING FOR EVERYMAN

He has, by the peculiarly potent chemistry of his nature and image, become the living symbol of an ideal that millions subconsciously would like to emulate, but realize would never work out for them in practice. He was every man's dreamland *alter ego* and every woman's dreamland *paramour*. The paradoxes in his makeup were all part of it--the swashbuckling toughness together with the poignant tenderness, the idolized hero and simultaneously, the small-boy underdog, the family man and yet the emancipated charmer of the world. This honesty, passion and vitality make up the essential elements of his singing.

*The Legend*

When you celebrate Sinatra, you celebrate the whole of him. It is his life that has created his artistic style, and he is a symbol of our lives – either factually or in fantasy. The audience knows he is both a luxuriating and a tortured soul, and therein lies the magic.

## His Life as Drama

What makes his life so enthralling? We know how people love to see success stories acted out, the poor-boy-makes-good saga; how they love to see the super-confident and loud-mouthed overreach themselves and fail, pride coming before the fall; how they love to see the conventional wisdom, which says "they'll never come back," overthrown and scorned, although not too often. Sinatra has acted out all these dramas, more than once, the very stuff of soap operas, and has thereby been the most striking exemplar in our lifetime of those two most common daydreams: the rise-and-fall story, and the come-back-against-the-odds story. This is what puts the final gloss of the champion upon him. Anyone who can so consistently overcome adversities that would sink lesser mortals, and, with equal persistence, snatch defeat from the jaws of victory, must be very special.

His chief producer from 1958 to 1961, Dave Cavanaugh, explained the perfection of "One For My Baby," the classic which rounded off "Only the Lonely." Sixty or seventy people were present, and Cavanaugh felt compelled to switch out the lights, all except for a spot. The atmosphere was exactly like a club as Cavanaugh set the tapes rolling, and the song was done in one take. That was "the only time I've known it to happen like that," said Cavanaugh, who explained on another occasion,

> Singing was like a lighting rod, particularly when he was in good voice; it discharged the hostile electricity. This stands as an archetypal great Sinatra performance—a man explaining his predicament to that most classic of all American father confessors, the after-midnight bartender. He does it naturally, vulnerably, universally, for the words are so cast that it's Everyman's hard-luck story. He sings like a master—hear how he varies the metric beat, hangs on to notes,

will even slip in an odd slur, ping or syllable that shouldn't, in a strict score sense, be there.

He's one hell of an actor too, and what a production Cavanaugh gives him. "The torch must be drowned…or it might soon explode," has him at his most broken-heartedly expressive. Cavanaugh concludes,"A husky patina envelope, the voice at times threatens to break, increasing the feeling of pain, and then it slowly fades, leaving the piano to an empathetic coda."

Sinatra brought to the long-playing record an artistry that could exploit the medium to its richest possibility. The whole emotional range of his singing had broadened and deepened, and that of course had sprung from the life he was leading. The message through these songs was about his failed marriage with Ava Gardner, and that could scarcely be clearer. The public could see that the affair was for real, not some showbiz fantasy, and that in some things neither men nor women can help themselves, however self-destructive the consequences.

Within two years of the 1953 release of *From Here to Eternity*, Frank had disproved the judgment of the pundits. Before that, he had lost his voice and his recording contracts were cancelled. He felt as if he were a failure and with that he experienced a great deal of depression. But then he had transformed himself into the most powerful force in Hollywood as an actor, recording star, and nightclub attraction. His enigmatic, chameleon-like ways, however, were often infuriating to those he worked with, as he once admitted to writer A.E. Hotchner with "I'm my own worst enemy."

So, should Sinatra desire to have a drink with friends after one of the shows, the 25-man security force, the D.A.'s guards, and Sinatra's own muscle guaranteed that no one was going to keep the drinks from flowing steadily from bar to table. No one, in fact, was going to get within thirty feet of the man. When the dozen or so friends were seated at the long rectangular table in the Galleria – Caesar's Palace's main wateringhole – a crowd would start to gather. When Jilly Rizzo, Barbara Marx, Pat Henry, and a few friends of the orchestra were congregated, the crowd would spot the one empty seat and would know.

The whispers begin. "Where is he?" "I think I saw him." "Yeah, he'll be coming out of that door there." Two Caesar's Palace guards move in.

## The Legend

"Move back. Keep to the rear. Don't block the way, huh." And then, as the recalcitrant are herded back, three men with sunglasses, surly stares, and the familiar bulge under the left arm position themselves by the entryway to the Galleria. This excites the crowd even more. Now they really know. Four more guards appear by the rear service door. The door opens a crack, and out comes Frank Sinatra.

The crowd, by now, is 100 strong. Frank Sinatra, surrounded by enough men to guard the President, takes his time sitting down. He does not look in the direction of the throng. That would be acknowledging the people, tantamount to saying, "I see you but I can't come over to say hello." He shouts to Jilly, who laughs, and then, snapping his fingers at a hotel manager, orders Sinatra's drink. And when Sinatra sits down, a full complement of security people moves in, one for every person at the table. They stand behind their charges, arms crossed like so many Colossi of Rhodes, giving everyone within range the Beady Stare. No one is going to mess with Frank Sinatra. (Vare, p.102).

Frank was adored around the world, and not just by Italian opera singers. The Japanese went nuts for him. The English abandoned their legendary reserve to give him standing ovations. The Europeans mobbed him. When he performed at the Concert for the Americas in the Dominican Republic in the middle of a steamy jungle, the Caribbean crowds were unbelievable.

But one area of the world in hich he was revered to an almost religious extent was South America, Rio de Janeiro in particular. When Sinatra performed at Rio's Maracana Stadium, more than 175,000 people made it an event that went into the Guinness Book of Records as the largest paying audience for a single performer. As Frank stepped onto that high center stage, the crowd exploded. The fans who had waited a lifetime went absolutely crazy, and the waves of noise that rippled from the far end of the stadium to the stage and back again almost knocked him off his feet. What a performance; his greatness was assured and his legend was in place.

Through it all, we may wonder how he got there. Now we'll look at the legend more closely.

CHAPTER TWO

# His Personal Calling

The American psychologist James Hillman first proposed the "acorn theory" in his book entitled *The Soul's Code: In Search of Character and Calling*. He suggested that every individual already holds his future potential inside himself from birth, just as the acorn already holds the pattern for growing into the oak tree. Each individual's unique energy becomes actualized through his choices and actions in life once he answers his life's calling, much like an acorn turns into an oak tree when it finally matures. (Hillman, 1997)

The myth says that the roots of the soul are in the heavens, and the human grows downward into life. A little child enters the world as a stranger, and brings a special gift into the world. The task of life is to grow down into this world. Little children are often slow to come down. Many children between the ages of approximately six to fifteen say, "I don't know what I'm doing in this family; I don't know how I ever landed here." Parents say about children, "Boy, I don't know where this child come from. He's nothing like anybody else in the family," and so on. From this perspective, we come into this earth as a stranger and slowly, as we mature, we grow into the world, take part in its duties and pleasures, and become more involved and attached.

"Sooner or later something seems to call us onto a particular path. You may remember this 'something' as a signal moment in childhood when an urge out of nowhere, a fascination, a peculiar turn of events struck like an annunciation: *This is what I must do, this is what I've got to have. This is who I am.*" (Hillman, 1997, p. 3)

What children must go through involves finding a place in the world for their specific calling. Extraordinary people display this calling most evidently. Perhaps that's why they fascinate us. Or, as Hillman believes, perhaps they are extraordinary because their calling comes through so clearly and they are so loyal to it. They serve as exemplars of calling and its strength, and also of keeping faith with its signals.

> Extraordinary people excite; they guide; they warn; standing as they do in the corridors of imagination—statues of greatness, personifications of marvel and sorrow—they help us carry what comes to us as it came to them. They give our lives an imaginary dimension. That's what we look for when buying biographies and reading the secret intimacies of the famous, their luck, their errors, their gossip. Not to pull them down to our level, but to lift ours, making our world less impossible through familiarity with theirs. (Hillman, 1997, p.32)

This idea has much to do with feelings of uniqueness, of grandeur and restlessness of the heart, its impatience, its dissatisfaction, its yearning. The heart wants to be seen, witnessed, accorded recognition. This was at the core of Sinatra's life and essence.

Maybe it's time to believe that each of us has a particular acorn, but that it is not always evident, that it is as unique as a fingerprint, and that the best way to succeed is to discover what you love and then find a way to offer it to others, allowing the energy within you to lead you.

I talked to a friend, Rosa Antonelli, a well-known concert pianist who has thought a bit about personal calling. She said that her initial motivation probably came from her mother, who was an opera singer:

> She was singing all the time during my childhood and so I felt connected to music right away. But in a mysterious way, I would say that it was the piano, itself. 'Mysterious' because something about the instrument attracted me immediately, even before I'd played it: you could say it was love at first sight.

## His Personal Calling

When I went to kindergarten, I saw a grand piano and told my mother that I wanted to play it. She said that after that I spent a lot of time looking at my hands and fingers with great fascination. I had already started dreaming about connecting myself, my fingers, with the instrument.

It was not easy for me to pursue my love of music as a child. I did not have my own piano to practice on until I was fourteen years old.

I remember how much I loved to practice: it was never enough; I always wanted to learn more and more pieces. When my teacher used to organize two or three recitals every year I was always chosen to perform, but of course she would notify my mother first. I remember that nothing else gave me more joy than when I was told that I would be playing in a concert. The happiest thing in the world for me was to perform and playing before an audience.

A very similar sentiment could have been uttered by Sinatra. We see that throughout his life up to late adolescence. He had dropped out of school and then saw no future for himself. He was trying to find a place in the world for his particular calling—what awaited his destiny. He had been struggling for some time to understand what kind of career he could follow. He remembered after seeing Bing Crosby in concert a signal moment that made its appearance to him. It struck him very clearly, and he then realized for the first time: "This is what I must do, this is what I've got to have. This is who I am." At that moment, he had a purer vision to guide him; and with that vision there was an infusion of desire that would power him in a certain direction.

He felt there was something unique about himself and he felt alive for the first time in his life He knew where he wanted, or had, to go. Hillman would say that his *daimon* kicked in and provided a clear path for his desire. Or maybe it was, as Sinatra would call it, "Lady Luck."

Could we believe that Sinatra might have been anything other than a singer? Did he know on some level that he had a voice that would enthrall a nation? There are so many questions we could ask relating to this and yet would it really afford us a clearer understanding of the path he took?

Did he know that he was unique and was destined to achieve artistic greatness? And if he knew this, at what point in his life did that thought make its appearance? Did he realize that he possessed this gift when he first sang with the Hoboken Five? He must have recognized this talent early on, which rendered it impossible for him to do anything other than be a singer. But we do know that when he got the position as waiter and singer at the Rustic Cabin, everything began to fall into place, and, with a bit of luck, the rest was history. At some point he knew he was destined for greatness.

Obviously, Sinatra was moved by his personal calling, much like other singers who knew this from an early age. He must have realized on some level that destiny had sought him out and given him this talent, and that it then was up to him to make the most out of it. And that is exactly what he did – he drove himself to the top of his profession.

He was careful to nurture this talent in himself, and thereafter he would enlist the help of the most talented musicians, composers, lyricists and arrangers. Possibly more than other singers, he treated his gift as if it were a present from the gods. Other singers did not value this ability in the same way. Throughout the turbulence of other parts of his life, he never treated his artistic life with anything less than immense reverence. Deep within, he knew that this unique gift had to be pampered, cared for, and loved.

Sinatra's career as a band singer, following his stint as a singing waiter at the Rustic Cabin, gave him his first taste of success. When Harry James left Benny Goodman and needed a singer for his new band, he signed Sinatra up to a two-year deal at $75 per week. A relentless road of one-nighters followed, but Sinatra received the exposure he craved. After all, a job with a popular big band was the end of the rainbow for a vocalist, or so it seemed in 1939. His association with Harry James allowed him to record his first hit, "All or Nothing at All," and receive favorable mention in George Simon's *Metronome* review of the band's performance at Roseland in New York City.

But as the popularity of the James band began to falter, Sinatra consciously planned his next move. Tommy Dorsey, who had the number-one band in the country, was to visit the Rustic Cabin and Sinatra arranged an "audition" by singing with Bob Chester's band that night. When Dorsey's featured male vocalist, Jack Leonard, left for a chance at a solo career, Dorsey offered Sinatra a contract and the twenty-four-year old singer knew that he had finally made it. And so he had. The Dorsey band was featured in the best venues around the country, often for weeks at a time, drawing large audiences and favorable press.

Just as important as this exposure, though, was the education in technique that Sinatra learned from the trombonist while being allowed to develop his style. Copying Dorsey's breathing technique, Sinatra recalled, "I was able to sing six bars . . . without taking an audible breath. That gave the melody a flowing, unbroken quality, and that's what made me sound different. When I started singing that way, people began taking notice."

Was it fate that brought Harry James into the restaurant, who then discovered Sinatra? And fate that would lead him to Tommy Dorsey, who made him an offer to come sing with his band? Within a short time, Sinatra knew he had to go out on his own, that he couldn't be held down by remaining as a band singer.

From there he was brought to Hollywood, and sang "Night and Day" in a cameo appearance in *Reveille with Beverly*. Even at the time, Sinatra's cameo didn't cause much of a stir, and *Reveille* doesn't feature in many official filmographies; it did mark in its modest way, though, the inception of Sinatra's solo career. It was a turning point for the young man and, of course, bigger changes were in the air.

## HE WAS DIFFERENT

Generally, at that time vocalists exuded little power; they would stand stiffly, smile, and sing the song. But when Sinatra's booking agency, GAC, persuaded the owners of New York's Paramount Theatre to add him to their big New Year's show, their driven young client had none of the star power of already signed performers like Benny Goodman and Peggy Lee. As Donald Clarke put it in *All or Nothing at All: A Life of Frank Sinatra* (1998), the Paramount Theatre was one of the shrines of the Swing era. When Sinatra was brought onstage in an almost desultory way by Benny Goodman, "the 28-year-old Francis Albert Sinatra stepped up, and history turned a small corner. He was met by a tsunami of hysterical screams from a group of young female fans. Goodman was initially thrown, completely struck dumb in fact, then looked over his shoulder and blurted out: 'What the fuck is that?' Sinatra laughed, and his fear left him."

Then his movie career blossomed when he discovered that he had an inherent acting ability, and this ability had much to do with his success as a singer. Obviously those who can act are able to infuse their lyrics with deeper emotion. For the next seven years, he was king of the universe– nothing could hold him back. In fact, he now reached out for the friendship and support of the Presidents of the United States from FDR to JFK, where he became an integral part of their inaugural ceremonies. With JFK, he had Sammy Cahn change the lyrics of "High Hopes" so that it was tailor-made for Kennedy.

When we look at Sinatra, we marvel at how this factor of fate showed itself, what it demanded of him, and how that fate finally became realized.

Extraordinary people are not of a different category; the workings of their internal engines are simply more transparent. Sinatra's life excites us; it fuels our own imagination. There may be more of an advantage in studying his extraordinary life, to learn about the depth of human nature, than by studying even a large sample of more ordinary lives. A single anecdote can light up a whole field of vision.

Take, for instance, the moment that Sinatra realized that he must leave Tommy Dorsey and go out on his own. Following his life, we are struck by a certain calling that became the essence of that life and constituted his destiny

Why are there so many biographies of Sinatra? Before you can make an accurate assessment, there may be two more being written. The reason must be that he fascinates us, that we love him and are excited by him. There are things about him that we would wish to emulate; he gives our lives an added dimension. He makes the world a richer place to live in; and we want to remain close to him because he lived life to its fullest and we wish we could borrow some of his enthusiasm. When we listen to his singing, we feel as if we are in a transformed state, romantic, sexy, uplifted, sad, mournful, lonely, and possibly waiting for life to reveal its more glamorous state. He pulls us in and enchants us; we want to stay close to people like him; there is an added dimension he gives to our lives.

What was there about him?— how he fought his way through opposition to do what he willed to do, against odds, probabilities, in order to practice a high art, to achieve a few moments of beauty that would delight the memory of those who watched, or listened, or read about him. What we mean by "legend" is what we mean by "art": the reaching of a form, a perfection, an appearance eternal in its beauty.

## THE PERSONAL CALLING IN OTHER SINGERS

Another picture of a personal calling relates to the female vocalist who many called the First Lady of Song—Ella Fitzgerald. From an early age, when she sang "A-Tisket, A-Tasket," her popularity and stardom were in place. When she was sixteen years old she entered the amateur night at the Harlem Opera House. She was announced to the crowd this way: "The next contestant is a young lady named Ella Fitzgerald . . . Miss Fitzgerald here is gonna dance for us . . . Hold it, hold it. Now what's your problem honey? . . . Correction, folks. Miss Fitzgerald has changed her mind. She's not gonna dance, she's gonna sing . . . " (Hillman, p. 10)

Ella Fitzgerald gave three encores and won first prize. Yet the announcer had initially thought she would dance and at the last moment she changed her mind. and then for the rest of her life she became one of the great interpreters of the American Song Book.

We need to ask ourselves, what changed her mind? Did a singing gene suddenly kick in? Or was it fate itself that pushed her to sing? The acorn had made its appearance.

In J.R.R. Tolkien's *Lord of the Rings*, we find Frodo wondering why he seems to have been chosen to carry the magical ring on such a perilous journey. Frodo wonders why he was such a man that he could effectively carry out such a daunting task. "But you have been chosen," Gandalfo says to Frodo, "and you must therefore use such strength and heart and wits as you have."

Growing up, Sinatra continued fighting to find a place in the world. Those who knew him early in life remember that he had a vague desire to become a singer. However the desire never became that pronounced, probably because he was never sure he could attain that dream or even have the talent to achieve it. In time, when he realized that maybe becoming a singer was not that much of a stretch of the imagination, he pursued it with all his might. His vision acted as a personal calling—he knew what he was meant to be, and the angels brought the vision into focus for him. Sinatra, being an extraordinary figure, displayed the idea of a calling more evidently than most. Perhaps this is why he fascinates us; and perhaps he is extraordinary because his calling came through so clearly and in turn he became loyal to it. It appears as if Sinatra had no other choice but to pursue the craft of singing.

Again, we have to repeat, could we imagine that he could have done anything differently than become a singer? He failed in school, his ability to hold down a job was erratic, but when he had the chance to sing with the *Hoboken Five,* something changed him, and when he saw Crosby at the theatre, he knew where his life had to go. Not so with Crosby.

## CROSBY AND SINATRA

We need to look at the lives of other singers, to see what we can learn from the similarities and differences in their stories, to show us how Sinatra's story is both similar and unique.

In the twentieth century, two musical figures stand out, Crosby and Sinatra, and each changed the way songs were vocalized. Crosby had racked up distinctions as a student of English, history, elocution, theology, Latin and civics. He was certainly the intellectually motivated student. Although he displayed varied talents, he never seemed to be driven to achieve in these areas. "Bing portrayed himself and was portrayed by others as an unambitious man to whom splendid things happened, deservedly, without his ever really chasing fortune." (Giddins, 1998, p.89).

In his freshman class, Crosby excelled in English, but it was really

## His Personal Calling

playacting and music that were becoming increasingly important to him, and he emerged as a school favorite. He was fourteen years old the first time he saw Al Jolson and was touched and excited by him. He thought Jolson was amazing; and he held a lifelong ambition to be able to hold a stage like Jolie.

He was taking law courses after college and joined the drama society. However, neither school nor drama diminished Crosby's appetite for music. He realized that his yearning for music would dominate all his other interests and, like Sinatra, he became obsessed with singing and performing, so that once he found his calling, he pursued it with all the vigor he had.

Like Sinatra, Crosby left a group and struck out on his own because the Rhythm Boys no longer were creating anything new, and he realized that the customers wanted to hear Bing himself. Crosby had represented something daring and refreshing in music, while the trio were doing the same thing over and over again, much like Sinatra's leaving the Dorsey band for slightly different reasons.

Crosby developed a style that was much more straightforward than that of other singers of his day. His voice was deep and masculine, and he appeared to be speaking straight to the listeners, unlike other singers who tended to belt out their songs. Crosby knew this, and it propelled him forward. Sinatra also was aware of how he would approach an audience with sex appeal, as if he were seducing someone.

We can follow the lives of other singers and find that each had this vision of himself, a calling that steered his lives in a particular direction.

Another popular crooner, Dick Haymes, achieved extraordinary success in the 1940's. He made the *Billboard* top-selling records and jukebox charts with more than fifty song hits in nine years. His own radio show and his contract with Twentieth Century-Fox, produced several popular film musicals, including the major success, *State Fair*. That, in addition to two films with Fox's leading screen goddess, Betty Grable, brought him to the pinnacle of Hollywood stardom. In 1946, Fox named Haymes as its top male box-office star, and he was in constant demand at nightclubs and theaters. *Motion Picture's* poll named Haymes "Hollywood's Crown Prince of Crooners" in 1946. Ten years later, he was all but forgotten as a film star, his recording career had ended, and he was bankrupt, owed alimony and child support, and had barely survived one of the worst media onslaughts ever directed against a celebrity in Hollywood history.

His mother, Marguertite Haymes, was probably the most powerful influence in the lives of her sons. When Dick was seventeen, he started singing on the beach and from then on couldn't stop singing. With his mother as his vocal coach, he gained fame, following Sinatra into the bands that he had left, notably the bands of Harry James and Tommy Dorsey. It does seem that singing was his calling in life and he pursued it with the same vigor as Sinatra. However, his career was impeded by too many personal problems, and in the end he did not nurture his talent, but rather watched it decline and fade away.

Tony Bennett recalls an incident that took place when he was three years old. His father took him to see one of the first talking pictures, *The Singing Fool*, in which the vaudeville star Al Jolson sang "Sonny Boy." He was so excited that he spent hours listening to Jolson and Eddie Cantor on the radio. At one of the family gatherings, he went into his aunt's bedroom and got her makeup. He covered his face with some white powder in an earnest attempt to imitate Jolson. Then he leaped into the living room and announced to the adults, who were staring at him in amazement, "Me Sonny Boy!" The whole family roared with laughter. He loved the attention and then he says that he felt as if he had been bitten by the showbiz bug.

Bennett, as well as his brother, loved music from this early age. After watching Bing Crosby and Maurice Chevalier, he had his mind set upon being a singer. He was also very talented in drawing and painting, and by the time he was ready to go to high school he had decided on pursuing a career in painting. A little later he discovered Frank Sinatra, whom he heard sing at the Paramount Theater. Thereafter, he started entering "amateur shows" in clubs all over Brooklyn, Queens and the Bronx, and started winning many of them.

When war broke out with Germany and Japan, Bennett volunteered for the Army and, while there, was recruited as a singer in the Army band. After leaving the Army and singing at an informal "musicale"

## His Personal Calling

every Friday night, he said that he was determined to become a professional singer and he persisted. He then secured Ray Muscarella as a manager who hired coaches for him, because he felt that Bennett needed some polishing. It was decided that if he didn't get a hit he would be dropped from the label he joined. And the rest was history, when Tony recorded "Because of You," which reached number one on *Billboard* magazine's pop chart on June 23, 1951. The song stayed on the chart for thirty-two weeks, ten weeks as number one.

Bobby Darin was one of the most charismatic performers in the 1960's and 70's. He could move with magical agility, could do great impressions, and was a swift and brilliant comedian. He was able to play seven instruments and could write fine songs–167 of them. He wanted to be a songwriter, actor, singer and musician and he became all of these. He appeared in 13 films and was nominated for an Academy Award in 1961 for *Captain Newman, M.D.* Darin knew from early adolescence that he was destined to be a singer and performer. He then spent the rest of his life developing this talent.

His rendition of "Mack the Knife" reached number one, where it would stay for nine weeks. It eventually sold over two million copies. Later, at the age of twenty-three, he became the youngest entertainer to ever headline in Las Vegas. He went on to win Grammys for the Best New Artist of the Year—the first-ever winner in that category—and for Record of the Year ("Mack the Knife"). Unfortunately, an early illness that recurred took his life at thirty-seven years of age.

Certainly, talent is a large part of one's calling. Each of these singers felt at an early age that that he wanted to spend his lives as a singer. Eddie Fisher starts his autobiography with these words:

> When I was a small child – I couldn't have been more than three or four years old – I opened my mouth and this beautiful sound came out and, for me, the world was changed forever ... That gift in my throat made me feel like a king – and caused people to treat me like one. It made me a star, one of the most successful singers in American history ... I had more consecutive hit records than the Beatles or Elvis Presley.

He then talks of meeting Presidents and says that his voice transformed him from a shy little boy into a man who attracted the most famous and desirable women in the world.

We see more clearly the prominence of personal calling when we look at the lives of these performers. There is a strong factor usually present that does not entail intelligence, talent or inheritance, but only motivation, which is the dominant theme in all these cases. These people display their calling most evidently – they have a vision of what they want to do in life and then spend their time reaching out and searching in order to attain that vision. These performers seemed to have no other choice – their fate was laid out before them.

How do we come to terms with our own uniqueness, our own impatience, dissatisfaction, our yearnings— and how do we come to terms with what destiny has given to us? What has fate provided for us, and how do we hear the call of destiny much the way Sinatra heard his? The myth that requires our understanding revolves around appreciating what it means to be born into this particular body; of these particular parents; and in such a place. We call these the external circumstances that form a particular unity. Further, we must contend with which influences had the greatest effect on our lives and how our character has directed our choices.

## EARLY SINATRA

Frank Sinatra came into the world a fighter and never let up. At birth, he was a huge baby, weighing 13 ½ pounds, and his mother was tiny, less than five feet tall. Worse, he lay in her womb in the breech position. The doctor, summoned to the Sinatra apartment in the Italian section of Hoboken, New Jersey on December 12, 1915, was forced to wage an excruciating tug of war with his forceps. Sinatra would have reminders of his birth – scars on the left side of his face and a punctured eardrum—for the rest of his life. And the battle wasn't over. Mistaking the seemingly lifeless infant for dead, the doctor concentrated on saving the baby's 20-year-old mother. But Frank had a determined maternal grandmother who wouldn't accept what seemed to be the inevitable. She scooped up her newborn grandson and held him under the cold-water tap until he began to bellow.

"The struggle of the infant would shape the character and conduct of the boy and remain a motivating force in the man," Sinatra's daughter, Nancy wrote later (1985).

"The household Sinatra was born into was typically Italian, with one notable exception. His mother wore the pants in the family. Although his husky dad, Anthony Martin Sinatra, had been a professional boxer, he was a meek man who took a backseat to his wife Natalie (better known as Dolly)."

By all accounts, everyone in Hoboken – a city just across the Hudson River from New York City, with the the Manhattan skyline in plain view – took a back seat to Dolly. "The mouth on that woman would make a longshoreman blush," recalled an acquaintance, Steve Capiello. Another friend remembered that Dolly's pet expression was "son of a bitch bastard."

It seems clear that Frank inherited from his mom the unrelenting feistiness that he would unleash uoon his enemies throughout his life. "Frank is like me," Dolly later admitted. "You cross him and he never forgets."

Frank spent most of his early years with the grandmother who had given him life. "It was lonely for me. Very lonely," he remembered. The difficult birth had precluded Dolly from having more children, which meant that Frank had no siblings, and she was too busy to care for him herself: "She was carving out a niche for herself in Hoboken politics."

Sinatra's school days were unexceptional. He had little interest in the subjects he was taught and finally decided to leave high school in his sophomore year. His mother had hopes that he would attend Stevens Institute of Technology, but he had no interest in that either. Somehow the idea of singing was lodged firmly in his mind, and he would spend a lot of his time learning songs off the radio.

From an early age, he had some hazy thoughts about being a singer. "The dream emerged unconsciously, perhaps merely as something that intrigued a lonely teenager, seeking in fantasies of fame a fulfillment and a revenge for what he could not find at home, in school or on the street," wrote biographer Arnold Shaw (1982). "It was easy to attract attention on summer nights by crooning the pop songs of the day under a lamp-post. His Hoboken pals apparently were not overwhelmed by his warbling."

Sinatra was a frail boy, never weighing more than 120 pounds. He would buy ice cream cones and candy for his cronies, who were usually beefy boys and good fighters. In return, they would protect their benefactor when the mischievous Frank got into frequent scrapes. They were the forerunners of the phalanx of bodyguard buddies who would later protect Sinatra.

His desire to sing strengthened his vision, and was something he felt he was driven to do, an inner urge that directed his life. In the beginning he began to imitate his idol, crooner Bing, by wearing hats and smoking pipes. When he placed a poster of Crosby on his bedroom wall, Dolly, who expected her son to go to college and become an engineer, had seen enough. She threw a shoe at him and called him a bum.

"In your teens," Sinatra later said, "there's always someone to spit on your dreams." But his dreams persisted, and when he attended a Crosby concert with girlfriend (and wife-to-be) Nancy Barbato in 1933, he vowed to her that he would make it as a singer.

Dolly's brother, Sinatra's uncle Domenico Garavanti, was the first to encourage the boy in a musical direction. Uncle Domenico's father had a tremendous voice, and when Frank was just a kid, all the relatives used to come out from Brooklyn and New York to Hoboken on a Sunday. There'd be lots of food and wine and Pop would sing. In fact, Dolly also used to sing at weddings and other family affairs. So Frank grew up with a lot of music around him. Once Uncle Dom bought Frank a ukulele for his fifteenth birthday and to everyone's surprise the young Sinatra mastered enough chord technique to strum an accompaniment to the Italian songs he heard at family gatherings. He may not have persuaded friends or relatives, but he was convincing himself that he had a voice, singing on the sidewalks in the evenings, or at beach parties on summer holidays with relatives. He was ready for the radio when it arrived in the Sinatra home, picking up the popular songs and learning them well enough to sing at his first concerts.

## His Personal Calling

In the beginning, his mother, who by now was resigned to this career path, arranged for him to sing for one or two dollars at gatherings of the Hoboken Sicilian Cultural League or the Democratic Party meetings. While in high school he made himself responsible for the hiring of musicians for school dances, and it was there that he had his first limited experience of singing with a band. A school friend recalls, "He didn't seem nothing more than a bag of bones in a padded jacket, but he was already making the girls turn around and watch him when he was there on the platform. He had a kind of style."

There were a few vocalists who were making their mark around this time, Al Jolson, Fanny Brice, Eddie Leonard, and Belle Baker. Radio was now breaking in, and NBC opened coast-to-coast broadcasting. CBS followed a year later; and a national, as opposed to state or city, audience was created, giving vocalists the exposure and the intimate listening conditions denied them by the big theatres or concert halls. Vocalists were on their way, and although the big bands continued to dominate popular music until the end of the Second World War, the best-known tunes were usually vocal numbers, especially those sung by Bing Crosby such as "Just One More Chance," and "I'm Through with Love."

### THE TURNING POINT

One March evening in 1933 the eighteen-year-old Sinatra took his girlfriend Nancy Barbato to hear Bing Crosby in a Jersey City vaudeville show. He left the Loews Journal Square theatre, turned to Nancy and told her, "I'm going to be a singer." And, back home that evening, he made the same statement of intent to his parents. "I saw Bing Crosby tonight and I've got to be a singer." The performance had excited, but not overawed, him. He was confident that he could hold his own with the best of them. His girlfriend and wife-to-be agreed with him.

Once Dolly saw that Frank couldn't be persuaded to give up his goal, she began to help him. She gave him money to buy an expensive sound system, then plunked down more cash so he could buy the latest orchestrations for the big-band songs he liked to sing. Sinatra, 17, would share his microphone and music with any band – provided they used him as their singer. While Frank continued his string of one-night stands with any band that would take him, he also befriended a local trio of singers, the Three Flashes. They were interested in Frank because he had a second-hand Chrysler car and was willing to chauffeur them to their gigs.

In 1935, the Three Flashes were summoned to audition for the famous *Major Bowes and His Original Amateur Hour*, a radio predecessor of *Star Search* that was broadcast nationwide. Once again, Dolly came to her son's aid by insisting that Frank be made part of the singing group. Who could say no to Dolly Sinatra? The Three Flashes became the Hoboken Four, and Frank Sinatra had made the first small step toward greatness.

In their first contest, the Hoboken Four won first prize. They garnered the biggest vote in the history of the show, with well more than 40,000 votes. Afterward, they were signed to begin a tour. But Frank couldn't stand the regimentation and left the tour before the end of the year. After that, he got a job at the Rustic Cabin roadhouse in Alpine, NJ. He both waited on tables and sang. Then, one night in 1939, Harry James walked into Frank's life. A trumpeter with Benny Goodman's band, James listened to the fledgling singer and was swept away. James later said that while watching Sinatra singing, he felt the hairs on the back of his neck rising and he knew that he was destined to be a great vocalist. The rest is history: from James he went on to Tommy Dorsey and then, after a successful number of years, took off on his own. His calling was now in place and his destiny secured.

Sinatra was determined to be different from Bing Crosby. He said that he sang more in the *bel canto* Italian mode of singing, which had to do with a flawless legato, perfect diction, and graceful phrasing, while based on a total mastery of breath control that fit him like a glove, He went on to describe how he had arrived at mastering these techniques.

Sinatra would always size up other singers. He praised Tony Bennett, who he felt was the best singer around, while with others he had reservations. He thought Vic Damone had the best "pipes" but he lacked the "know-how: or whatever you wanted to call it, and thought Lena Horne was a beautiful lady but really a mechanical singer. He was always impressed by Ella Fitzgerald, but he favored Sarah Vaughn, whom he saw as a superior singer. And then he was impressed with Peggy Lee and the way she interpreted a song. The point is that Sinatra carefully studied other singers and analyzed their performances; however he never seemed to compete with them or be concerned about their success.

He mentioned that he got about 500 new songs a year sent to him, and that chances were 497 of them wouldn't be too good. But he looked at them anyway. He basically studied the submissions for the continuity of melody that in itself would tell a musical story. The lyrics must tell you a complete story, he believed, so that the artist is able to sing the song properly; and that is when the audience pays attention to every note and every word. (Kaplan, 2005)

Sometimes celebrities seem like displaced persons, always needy, and haunted by an unspoken tragedy that is blamed on parents or betrayals in love, or even forced and inhumane schedules. Addictions that keep stars estranged and "out of it," suicide attempts, and early death may result from the conflicts between personal goals and life itself, a feeling that the world demands too much of them. Hillman (1997, p. 198) The life of Judy Garland exemplifies these issues.

## THE LIFE OF JUDY GARLAND

Garland was born in 1922 into a show-business family that promoted her almost as soon as she could stand up. Her original name was Frances Gumm, and when as a child she sang solo and the audience roared approval, she responded and almost refused to get off the stage.

At two years of age, she knew exactly what she wanted to do in life. She said that what she did just came naturally, because no one ever taught her what to do on stage. As an adult, she came into immense fame and adulation was her due. Fred Astaire said that she was the most talented woman he ever knew. She acted in some very poignant films such as *The Clock* (1945) and *Judgment at Nuremberg* (1961), but the movie she will always be remembered for is *The Wizard of Oz* (1939) and, of course, the song that came out of that movie, which was her signature piece, "Somewhere Over the Rainbow."

The critic Clifton Fadiman was able to see the essential features of Garland when he wrote:

> As we listened to her voice…as we watched her, in her tattered tramp costume…we forgot – and this is the acid test of who she was, and indeed who we were ourselves. …She had no "glamour," only magic. She expressed a few simple, common feelings so purely that they floated about in the dark theatre, bodiless, as if detached from any specific personality. (Hillman, 1997, p. 51)

Most of us never reach the heights of a Garland, yet she always wanted to enter the regular world, to live with a man in a stable marriage. But what kept her going was none of these normal outcomes but the ruthlessness of her vision, which opposed them. She did not know how to keep house, be married, raise children, cook a meal, or make anything with her hands. She remarked once, "Maybe it's because I made a certain sound, a musical sound, a sound that belongs to the world. But it also belongs to me because it comes from within me." (Hillman p. 53 )

Garland believed her calling "was inherited. Nobody ever taught me what to do on stage . . . I just did 'what came naturally.'" Remembering her initial "Jingle Bells" performance, she compared the rush onstage to "taking nineteen hundred wake-up pills." The Garland of the Hollywood Bowl and Carnegie Hall was already present in two-year-old Baby Gumm.

In many ways, Sinatra and Garland are similar. The conditions of nostalgia, sadness, silence, and a yearning imagination are the stuff of their songs, their voicing and phrasing, their body language, and their face and eyes. It is no wonder that their performances reached the common heart as no others did. They made each of their listeners aware of what he or she, too, most intimately longed for: they awakened the image in the heart of their fans a yearning for what was not in this world.

Both Garland and Sinatra were born with a particular gift. But talent is only a piece of their calling; many are born with musical, mathematical, and mechanical talent, but only when the talent serves the fuller image and is carried by character do we recognize exceptionality. Many have talent, but few are chosen; therefore, many have talent, though few have the character that can realize that talent. Character is a mystery, and it is different in each individual.

Musicians and people who follow show business know that Marian Anderson gave her first paid performance at eight; Mozart, as a child, could hum any tune he heard. It was not simply the pronounced calling to show business that led them to their heights; as in the case of Garland and Sinatra, it was also the character with which each of them performed his calling. In essence then, character is not what one does but the way one does it.

## LONELINESS

The stories of both Sinatra and Garland tell of solitude in the midst of world acclaim. How do we account for the loneliness that accompanies every life? Loneliness belongs to childhood. That loneliness in a child's heart may be aggravated by fears of the dark, punishing parents, or rejecting friends. Its source, however, seems to be the solitary uniqueness that inhabits the psyche of each individual. It needs to be expressed and to find its way through all facets of creative action.

The conditions of nostalgia, sadness, loneliness, and yearning imagination are the stuff of both Garland's and Sinatra's songs. No wonder that their performances reached the common heart as no others did.

When we look more closely at both Sinatra and Garland, we can begin to understand as well how they were able to keep their fans and professional admirers despite their erratic behavior, their petulance, and their hostility. They made each of their listeners aware of what they, too, most intimately were longing for: the awakened image in the heart of the displaced person and his/her yearning for what was not in this world.

At this point in considering Sinatra's life, our interest lies less in his personality than in the remarkable factor of fate itself – how it arrives and shows itself, what it demands, and its side effects. We look at the movement of his life for evidence of manifestations of destiny. It would seem that his life was formed by an unique image, an image that called his life to its destiny, which can be referred to as his personal calling. He couldn't be anything other than what he became, as he was motivated to pursue his dream, which certainly served him well and guided him throughout his life.

In January 1942, *Billboard* named Frank Sinatra as top band vocalist. Sinatra had also moved Bing Crosby out of the top of the *Downbeat* popularity poll that Crosby had occupied for six years. Sinatra said in retrospect that he didn't want to be number one. "I knew that was Bing Crosby. But somebody had to be number two."

Right from the beginning, and in an early album, he was called "the Voice." What does it really mean to be called that, as if there were no other voices? Everyone knew he had that special something and that it was only time before it would evolve, and when it did, the world was awakened to his magical presence.

It was clear that his was more than a new voice, it was a different voice. He was the spark that ignited a teenage revolution. Yes, the Voice was born and destiny had its way.

When he decided to go out on his own he told Joey D'Orazio, "I'm gonna be the biggest singer in the business, as big as they come." This was a familiar refrain. He said the same thing to Sammy Cahn, among others. When Sammy Cahn agreed, telling him, "There is no way anything can get in your way," Sinatra was filled with an almost overwhelming sense of empowerment. "You do believe, then, don't you?" he asked Cahn, excitedly grabbing his arm. Certainly Sinatra believed in his own potential. He became excited when he was able to convince others, and with his prodigious talent, that wasn't difficult to do.

Nick Sevano, a friend of Sinatra's,, said: "Nothing meant anything to him but his career." Sinatra's first wife, Nancy, in describing Frank's determination to succeed, said,

> "Oh, Frank always had it... Before he even joined Harry... he was focused, which you know is important, and it took a lot of work. He used to be very tired when he got through working because he put everything he had into it. But without Tommy I know it still would have happened... Frank had a master plan for himself, and he worked at getting there. I think he always had it in the back of his mind that this was a stepping stone." (Sinatra, N., 1986)

CHAPTER THREE

# The Productive Narcissist

There are few subjects of greater interest than what it takes to excel and reach the apex of success. What kind of people become world-class performers or even athletes and scientists? Is there something motivationally special about those who make it to the top? It is often assumed that this special motivation is the prerequisite to excellence in all areas of human endeavor. Do these people possess a different sense of self, and/or do they perceive their options differently?

The term "narcissism" has entered our language, referring to negative character traits. It has meant a broad assortment of self-absorbed, self-centered behaviors. In other instances, it may connote a kind of vanity, an overwhelming preoccupation with one's own image and the constant need for the admiration and attention of others. We relate the idea of narcissism to a picture of someone who is arrogant, haughty, grandiose, thinks he or she is superior and deserving of special treatment, someone who requires excessive admiration, is oblivious to the feelings of others, takes advantage of them, lacks empathy, and can be snobby, disdainful, or patronizing.

At times, Sinatra could embody some of the above qualities; however, there were certainly other aspects of his personality that make this assessment too one-sided. He was much more complicated, and it is important to understand the complexities of his success.

Essentially, the term narcissism can also highlight a personality type, and, like any other personality, it can be productive or unproductive, creative or destructive, healthy or sick, generous or selfish. Narcissism should not be used as a synonym for bad manners or rude, self-centered behavior. Certainly Sinatra has been seen to represent many of the above characteristics; and in this sense he would be seen as a narcissist. However, the term could also characterize other more dynamic aspects of his personality.

Maccoby (2003) sees narcissists as people who feel that there are fewer social restraints placed upon them than upon others. They may be less worried about losing love or bending to peer pressure. Or, to put it another way, they may not be concerned about doing the right thing and, in this manner, they have fewer internal constraints: ultimately, they are forced to answer to themselves for what is right, to decide what they value, what gives them a sense of meaning. So they do not have to look for approval from others, do not hear the chorus of voices that say, "You're a good boy, keep it up." There is no need to follow in their father's footsteps or to take over the family business. And the way they achieve a sense of security differs from that of others. Narcissists recruit people to join them in their worldview and their vision, so that they can feel a sense of security and overcome isolation. For this reason, narcissists are driven to be captivating, inspirational, charming, and seductive.

Narcissists must create their own sense of meaning, their own sense of purpose, a mission that first engages their passion and then engages others. In this sense, they don't buy into the meaning offered by parents or peer groups, so that they feel little pressure to fit in or conform as children to the other kids. This is a major reason why Sinatra could say to his parents that he wanted to be a singer and then be able to brush aside their criticisms and personal attacks. He had to follow his own path in spite of any doubts that others might have expressed. At crucial times, Sinatra went up against the authorities, who believed that he may not have possessed the talent needed to take him on this particular roller coaster ride.

More often, the picture of the productive narcissist is applied to successful CEOs who feel that they want to change the way things have been going, or simply change the world. And they feel that they are in a position to change it: they don't just react to the external world, but they want to alter it to the way they think it should be going.

This fits with much of the essence of Sinatra's life: he was drawn to creating his own sense of meaning and didn't react to the external world so much as he tried to create it. He dropped out of high school and then decided that he wanted to be a singer against the advice of his parents, who were furious with him. He then pursued his vision and finally was able to recruit his mother, Dolly into helping him. From Harry James he went to Tommy Dorsey, and then decided to leave to go on his own. He brought in a superior team of agents, composers, and lyricists to further his development. He picked his own material and had very particular ideas of how his arrangements should develop. Even though he revered Nelson Riddle, he would constantly berate him for not following strict orders, until Riddle couldn't take it anymore and severed his ties, only to be reunited some years later.

When Sinatra decided that he wanted to play the role of Maggio, nothing could stop him from getting the part. He entered into a conflict with Capitol Records, so he decided to start his own label. These are just a few highlights of his career, but they certainly confirm the idea that Sinatra was a supreme, and productive narcissist.

As mentioned before, a narcissist can be either productive or unproductive. The ones who are unproductive don't really move too much in life; they are not motivated to succeed. However, the ones who are productive like Sinatra are the ones who make a decided difference and have the charisma and drive to convince others to buy into their vision. They communicate a sense of meaning that inspires others to follow them, whereas the unproductive types withdraw into their own world. The productive ones are the people who take the risks that others can't or won't dare to take. They transform our world through the arts and of course through politics, business and social action.

Freud recognized that there is a central engine of self, a part of our personality that is shaped by forces that are hard-wired into our unconscious. This part forms our core personality, and it becomes the typical, habitual way we relate to the world, control and direct our passions, and shape and discipline our talents. Unlike other personality types, the narcissist as a core personality is forced to answer for himself what is right, to decide what he values, and what gives him a sense of meaning.

The most common family dynamic shared by productive narcissistic personalities is the presence of a strong, supportive mother and an absent or failed father. Sinatra's own father, Marty, was basically ineffectual. Without an admired father figure, or without a father who is a strong and positive presence, a narcissistic child, especially a boy, is free from paternal domination, someone to measure himself against or live up to. His major encouragement and affirmation comes from a supportive mother.

Sinatra's tenacity, drive, and cunning owe a lot to his mother Dolly, who always had her eye on the main chance; in her time, she was both a midwife and an abortionist, a local politician and a Prohibition saloonkeeper. "She was the force!" Sinatra said. She always could find a way to do what she wanted to do, and get everyone to go along with it.

John D. Rockefeller's father was quite literally a snake-oil salesman who was on the road most of the time, peddling his products in different towns, until he finally left his family for another woman. Leonardo da Vinci was an illegitimate child who was later reunited by his birth father at age five, and Leonardo remained close to his natural mother throughout his life. The mother of William Durant, the founder of General Motors, was a divorced, single parent, something unusual at the turn of the century, who doted on Willie and supported him in everything that he did. Durant's father was a hard-drinking, get-rich-quick guy who was shunned by his family.

Think also of Duke Ellington, whose elegant and strong-willed mother supported and encouraged his musical genius, while Ellington's father worked as a servant in the White House. Also, Douglas MacArthur's mother encouraged and promoted his military career, sticking close by him throughout his career to make sure he was measuring up to her standards. When he was at West Point, she lived in a nearby apartment; she even followed him when he was shipped out to the Philippines, renting out a room in a hotel. Frank Lloyd Wright's mother Anna decided, before he was born, that he would be the greatest architect in the world. She wanted the first images he saw as an infant to inspire him, so she placed engravings of great cathedrals around his crib. His toys were wooden building blocks, all to encourage his architectural talents. Nelson Riddle, Sinatra's major orchestrator, remarked that both Sinatra and himself were only children born into families with dominating mothers and retiring fathers. From the beginning of their lives, feelings of loneliness became a dominant emotion.

Stephen King, one of the most productive and successful American writers, had no father from the age of two, but his mother was a strong presence in his life. And of course our two Presidents, Barack Obama and Bill Clinton, grew up without the presence of a father, and yet each reached the pinnacle of success and power.

Not having a strong father as a role model, narcissists train themselves from an early age to block out other voices, other opinions, so that one of the few voices they trust is their own. They talk exclusively to themselves. Shakespeare recognized this when he created literature's greatest monologist, Hamlet. To quote Harold Bloom: "Hamlet, in his seven soliloquies, teaches us what imaginative literature can teach, which is how to talk to oneself, and not how to talk to others. Hamlet is not interested in listening to anyone, except perhaps the Ghost."

Often productive narcissists are consumed by a passion and they seem possessed by an inner god, a drive, that enlivens and elevates the everyday to the extraordinary and acts as a dynamic energy, a sense of freshness that energizes their work. Without this passion or enthusiasm even the most skillful, focused, reasoned and talented person can just go through the motions at work, passively accepting tasks as if they were assignments. Passion is what makes the difference between the talented singer who just phones in the role and the highly productive one, who is able to bring all of his talents to bear in his work and remake each song with fresh insight.

Another element of productiveness is the quality of perseverance. Those who are productive simply do not give up, even when faced with defeat or failure. They are resilient. The quality of perseverance is what pushes any personality type to live up to its potential. Sinatra pushed his personality to the limit, animating all he did with the spark, the inner drive, that elevated his work.

Of all the singers in his time, Sinatra was the most productive. He was an independent thinker who acted out of freedom even when it meant taking big risks. He was motivated by a vision of bringing new meaning to his music. He used everything he could, including the most talented of people, to implement his vision, learning as much as possible along the way. He was energized, even obsessed, by his vision, charismatically drawing others into his internal dialogue. He knew exactly who was with him and who was against him, and became very alert to threats. And finally, he was emotionally connected to the real world.

Vision is the key to understanding Sinatra's creative and productive stance. Once he found his purpose, his vision, it crystallized his strengths. His passion flamed up, bringing his talents and skills to life. Passion is purpose. There were many other singers with wonderful skills, but they lacked a broader vision.

Sinatra had an undeniable emotional pull on others. He was a big charmer and very resilient. He learned to rebound, rather than give up. He suffered the kind of defeats that would have left other personality types cowering under their covers for years, but refused to acknowledge or even register those defeats. There is no such thing, for example, as an American President who is humble and shy; it takes drive and tough resolve in order to succeed in both business and politics, and this could also be said about making it in the entertainment business.

In all his interviews, Maccoby (2003) found that successful narcissists continually used words such as disciplined, rigorous, dogged, determined, consistently focused, accountable and responsible. In short, they primed themselves for their upward success and their drive to excel.

The narcissist becomes productive only when he or she develops a passion to achieve something. Sinatra changed when he saw that audiences really got excited about his singing, and the major change occurred with his startling engagement at the Paramount.

After he joined the Dorsey band, he phrased his voice to be like the way Tommy played. "I could tell the difference in his singing in just a few weeks," Jo Stafford said. She added that Frank just happened to have a wide rib cage just like Tommy's. (Kaplan, 2005).

In time, Dorsey would become more than Sinatra's musical mentor – he became a hero and a father figure to him. Sinatra asked Dorsey to be the godfather of his first child, Nancy. He also picked up on some of

Dorsey's personal traits: his impatience; his insistence on exerting a firm control over every situation; his demands to achieve and maintain perfection; his largesse in helping friends and those in extreme distress; his habit of treating longtime employees with disdain, while constantly testing both their efficiency and their loyalty; his enjoyment of playing the dedicated host; his spendthrift ways, which didn't always carry over to the paychecks of his underlings; his natural charm (which could be followed by abrupt mood swings); his constant search to associate himself with upper-class people, while in the long run finding that he was more comfortable with his own peers; the vengeance aimed at his enemies; and a complete inability to apologize for his actions, even when confronted with the fact that he was wrong.

Before Henry Ford started his own company, he always worked for someone else. However, when he started experimenting with internal combustion engines in his own home he knew, all of a sudden, what he wanted to do: build the "universal car" for the "great multitude." So, once Ford discovered his purpose as well as his vision, he pursued it with nothing short of absolute clarity. We could say something similar about Sinatra after he went to see a performance by Bing Crosby. His future wife heard him say that singing is what he had to do, and this is who he was. Nothing then could stop him.

What Sinatra had going for him was an ability to inspire others. This applied to agents, arrangers, composers, and songwriters. They would become his devoted followers. Robert Asprey (2002) writes about Napoleon in a similar way. "No commander in history has so inspired his troops to march, often without adequate food or wine, on occasion without shoes, frequently with meager clothing in dreadful weather. Time and again . . . he asked his men to do what appeared impossible – and they did it."

And underneath it all narcissists are blessed with this infectious charisma, and they have an undeniable emotional pull on others. In addition, they are big charmers. They need their followers much the same way that politicians need their audience, their constituency. Think of some of our presidents – Lincoln, FDR, Reagan, and Clinton, who have been extraordinary communicators and charmers, and could be seen as productive narcissists.

These people feed off the admiration of others, becoming ever more spontaneous and more sure of their message. Not enough is understood about why Sinatra needed an entourage that followed him after his concerts. The entourage felt excited to be included in the "Sinatra group," and their reaction often topped that of Hollywood actors and actresses. When Sinatra was scheduled to perform for a charity function at the Sphinx in Egypt, he sent out invitations to many stars including Cary Grant. Grant had doubts about wanting to make the trip; however the thought of not going bothered him, possibly because he felt that he would face ostracism by Sinatra afterward.

Sinatra was planning to host a large charity function in Las Vegas and sent out invitations to many celebrities with suggested amounts to contribute. Among those celebrities was Tarkanian, the coach of the University of Las Vegas basketball team. He came home to his wife and told her about the invitation and then went on to say that the contribution he was expected to make would amount to almost 20 percent of his yearly salary. His wife then asked him what he was going to do. He looked at her and said, "Do I have a choice?" What he meant was that he was afraid of what Sinatra could do to influence the fans coming to the games, and he was building a team that needed as many attending fans as possible.

The productive narcissist impresses others as being "a personality." Narcissists have the ability to inspire others, to take on the role of leader, and they are the type of people who are most likely to say that they want to change the world, to inject new meaning into their careers. They reject how things are for how things should be. Narcissists do not react to the external world so much as they try to create it. They rarely listen, because the narcissist's vision always starts with a rejection of the *status quo*. They have a precise vision of how things should be and they are able to communicate a sense of meaning that inspires others to follow them. People such as Bill Gates and Opray Winfrey would fit that category. They are able to create new visions and motivate others, and in this endeavor they transform our world.

Erich Fromm, the noted psychologist, sees productivity as the ability to use our powers and to realize the potentialities inherent in ourselves.

The empowered person experiences himself as the embodiment of his powers and as the "actor." But it is passion that is the juice that brings the other elements of productiveness to life. Without this passion or enthusiasm, even the most skillful, focused, reasoned, and talented person can just go through the motions at work. It is productivity that pushes any person to live up to his potential. So when we say that Sinatra was productive, we mean that he was able to move his ability to its highest level. He used everything he could to implement his vision. He was energized by this vision, charismatically drawing others into his internal dialogue

Sinatra became a productive narcissist only when he developed a hunger for singing along with the desire to alter the way songs were delivered. He became energized, came out of his deep funk when he saw that people were moved by his performance. He created an entirely new approach to delivering a song, and this in turn ignited the eagerness that became a mission statement for his future. There was a constant bubbling up of new ideas that needed to be tested and tried out, and then his singing took off.

At that time, his personal life suffered because his work was his life. This kind of constant and passionate devotion is what brings about change, but it can be brutal in regard to one's family. Sinatra was consumed with working, recording songs, playing concerts, and then acting in movies. However, there were other less attractive traits that he exhibited, especially his arrogance.

## Arrogance and Aggression

Freud wrote that a narcissist's ego has a large amount of aggressiveness at its disposal. Sinatra was known for his outbursts and eruptions over the smallest of mistakes, such as a lack of attention to detail by one of his colleagues. While other types of personalities may yell or abuse their staff, they usually don't have as much free-floating aggressive energy. And this aggression was always on the surface for him, readily available.

Sinatra was one of those individuals who could be both verbally and physically abusive. The first indication of this was in his relationship to

Buddy Rich, the eminent drummer with Tommy Dorsey. Sinatra and Buddy Rich were in fierce competition, because Rich resented the prominence that Sinatra was achieving within the band. One hot evening at the Astor Roof, Sinatra was crooning a ballad when Rich abruptly departed from the feathery beat he had established with the brushes and started playing loudly with his sticks, throwing off Sinatra's delivery and destroying the romantic mood of the song.

When Sinatra came off the bandstand, Rich started cursing him and Sinatra picked up a pitcher full of ice water from a table next to him and threw it at Rich. Fortunately, Buddy ducked and the pitcher crashed into the wall.

The night after the incident, Dorsey sent Sinatra home. This was the first of two firings of his tempestuous band singer. A few nights later, as Rich was leaving the Astor, he was approached by two hoodlums, one of whom asked, "Is your name Rich?. . . We're friends of Frank," before they proceeded to mug him. The front-page story, emblazoned on the September 1, 1940 issue of *Downbeat,* declared "Buddy Rich Gets Face Bashed In," reporting that it "looked as if it had been smashed in with a shovel."

Very few successful people would have ever resorted to this kind of violence. Afterward, it was Sinatra himself who would sock another person. For example, Lee Mortimer had a thing against Frank and would criticize him in his columns. One night at a nightclub, Frank confronted Mortimer and then punched him in the mouth, and when he crumbled to the floor, Frank got on top of him and punched him some more, calling him ugly names. He settled when Mortimer sued him for $9,000.

On another occasion, Sinatra escorted Judy Garland to a nightspot, and when someone uttered some words that Frank did not like, he threw the guy into a telephone booth and punched him out.

There was an instance when Frank was in a restaurant together with Ava Gardner and Sam Giancana. Ava never felt comfortable around Giancana, so she got up and walked over to a man who was at a table alone. She began to flirt with him, touching his arm and rubbing the back of his neck, and then climbing onto his lap. Frank became furious and got up and went over to the stranger's table. He pushed Ava off the man's lap, and then pulled the stranger up by his collar, looked him straight in the eye, and in a voice loud enough to be heard over the music said, "You're lucky I don't kill you with my bare hands, you idiot. Who the fuck do you think you are? Are you crazy? You want to die? Because I'm the guy to make that happen, you chump." When Frank finally released his grip, the guy fell to the floor. (Kaplan, 2015).

Obviously, Frank had trouble controlling his aggression, which is possibly the reason he liked to be around Giancana, a noted gangster. Frank knew that Giancana would resort to rubbing out people and it was said that he killed many of his opponents. Of course, we would like to ask why Frank would find that so enticing, but he did. And that is where narcissists can get into major trouble. Their grandiosity, their inflated sense of who they are, and their over-evaluation of their power makes them a threat to those who get in their way.

## HUMOR

One of the most underrated and most important positive characteristics of productive narcissists is a sense of humor, especially about themselves. Sinatra was not known to have such a sense of humor, although he could laugh at himself infrequently. On stage, his humor often consisted of putting down actors or actresses that he had played with in a movie. One occasion comes to mind when he was performing at Radio City Music Hall, and he took off and belittled Kathryn Grayson, with whom he had appeared in a few movies. While the audience laughed at his remarks, they really weren't that funny.

On another occasion, he had been asked to see this new comedian, Don Rickles, by Rickles' mother, and he had agreed to it. So he entered the club where Rickles was performing with an entourage of friends. As they entered the club, Rickles, who was on stage, spotted him and threw off these lines: "Hey Frank, make yourself comfortable, hit someone." The group who was with Frank stopped in their tracks, not knowing how to respond unless they got the cue from Frank, and Frank howled, at which time the rest of people cracked up also. But it was clear that this entourage was careful about how they should react.

In yet another instance, Frank was shooting *Come Blow Your Horn*. He sounded off one afternoon while they were filming, which of course stopped the movie from progressing. The director, Yorkin, was told the next morning that Frank wanted to talk to him. So he went into his dressing room and Frank told him to sit down and then said, "Bud let me ask you something. Did anyone ever tell you that I might be difficult to work with?" Yorkin nodded his head, "Yeah, I heard that." Frank went on, "Did anybody ever tell you that I don't like to do a lot of takes and so forth?" Then Frank said, "Have you ever heard that when five o' clock comes, it's martini time? We could be right in the middle of a scene, but it's over for me, because it's martini time. Did you ever hear that?" Yorkin agreed that he had heard it. "Well jeez, if you heard all that, why didn't you get Howard Keel to play the role?"

Yorkin broke up. Sinatra did too. Frank clapped his hands and together they went back to work, doing it mostly Frank's way. Yorkin realized how careful you had to be when talking to him.

It was obvious that Frank got a big kick out of the number of roasts in which people made fun of him, but he already knew he was in a friendly and respectful atmosphere, and none of the jokes was too personal. And of course there was his rowdiness while in a performance of the Rat Pack. However, he was acting in this role, and in his movies he could be funny. But as Yorkin said, you had to be careful.

Similarly, Frank Loesser had trouble with the way Sinatra was singing "Sue Me," from *Guys and Dolls*. He approached Frank and told him that he would like to speak to him about this, and offered to meet him in his bungalow; but Sinatra asked him to come to his dressing room. When Loesser came there, it was filled with many people and loud noises. So he said to Sinatra, "How the hell can we discuss anything in this atmosphere?" Sinatra did not want to hear anything about his delivery on the song so he said to him, "We'll do it my way or you can fuck off." Actually, he never forgave Frank Loesser for telling him how to play Nathan Detroit.

It was difficult to know how Sinatra would react to any kind of criticism, but one must consider that Loesser was one of the most prominent composers of his time and he did indeed write both the music and lyrics to *Guys and Dolls*.

## GRANDIOSITY AND SENSITIVITY TO CRITICISM

As we've seen from his earliest days, Sinatra was extremely sensitive to any kind of criticism. In the beginning, while he was singing at the Rustic Cabin, Joey D'Orazio, one of Sinatra's friends, told him that he wasn't bad but his singing could use some work. He said it in a friendly way and thought he was being helpful. But Frank became insulted. "Fuck you and your whole family," he said. "If you can't pay a guy a decent compliment don't be comin' around here. Whatcha think I need, you tearin' me down?" Either you were with him or you were against him—that was Frankie.

Sinatra was almost hard of hearing when it came to criticism, wherever it came from. Sammy Davis, at an interview when asked about Sinatra, said, "Talent is not an excuse for bad manners. I don't care if you are the most talented person in the world. It does not give you a right to step on people and treat them rotten. This is what he does occasionally." When Frank heard what he said, he wrote him out of the movie *Never So Few* and then refused to talk to him for years afterward, even when Sammy begged him for forgiveness.

The disc jockey Jonathan Schwartz is one of Sinatra's most ardent fans. He plays his music constantly and seems to have molded his life around Sinatra's. It would be hard to think of another individual who was as committed to Frank. Yet when Sinatra put out his *Trilogy* album, Jonathan made some very slight criticisms of it. Sinatra called him in the early morning and lambasted him, calling him most vile names. Of course, Jonathan was totally devastated; and then it was years before Frank would forgive him and let him into his circle, since they both had homes in Palm Springs.

He was known to write out close friends from his life if he sensed there was an iota of criticism coming his way.

## GRANDIOSITY

Narcissists feel entitled to live in a grand manner; and certainly Sinatra epitomized this with homes throughout the country and, of course, a private jet at his disposal. Barbara Sinatra tells this story.

When we arrived anywhere, Frank would hand Jilly a stack of hundred-dollar bills and say, "Take care of all the busboys and waitresses." His tipping was legendary, especially to the little guys. At one restaurant we went to, we were waiting for our car afterward and Frank handed the valet who parked the car two hundred-dollar bills.

"Thank you, Mr. Sinatra!" the kid cried delightedly.

"Is that the biggest tip you ever had?" Frank asked.

The young man looked coy. "Well, no, sir."

Frank frowned. "What the — ? Who the hell gave you more than that?"

"Why you did, Mr. Sinatra. Last week."

He was without fail, warm, gracious and giving. Everywhere he went he'd stop to buy extravagant gifts for friends and family, shipping parcels home or having surprise packages and flowers delivered to their rooms. He remembered everything, from friend's favorite colors to what kinds of cologne they wore. He addressed store and hotel staff by their first names, recalling them from previous visits. He led Nancy into a jewelry shop and almost bought the place out. He chose to buy his wife, Barbara, some beautiful earrings and a ring and then went back on his own to buy something else, telling her, "You'd look maaarvelous in this!"

## Motivation

Most would agree that certain motivational characteristics are, indeed, critical components of outstanding achievement. Making it to the top in almost any area of endeavor possibly does require certain of these characteristics. A general conclusion that was reached in Benjamin Bloom's (1982a, 1982b) research on world-class performers in a wide range of areas found that this something called "motivation" distinguished those who managed to excel. Ability and opportunity were certainly necessary components, but they were not sufficient. There was something motivationally special about world-class athletes, pianists, outstanding artists, scientists and mathematicians.

One characteristic that seemed to emerge in many interviews with high achievers was that they were very goal-oriented and highly confident of their own ability, regardless of the area in which they happened to excel. It was also interesting to find that high-achieving business people, scientists and artists had more in common than could have been guessed. They talked about themselves and their careers in ways that were not dissimilar.

In interviews, these achievers stressed the importance of believing in oneself. They expressed the idea that only those who had a high degree of confidence could possibly manage to excel. One businessman stressed the particular theme that to be successful, one had to have self-confidence that "borders on arrogance." Clearly, the will to succeed is one aspect of productive narcissists. They do not need to boast to assure others – or themselves – that they are good. They simply express the strong belief that they are people who can do what has to be done, and will do it right. They see themselves as an élite class, excelling over their peers in almost every way. They also see themselves as setting standards that were uniquely their own. As one of them put it in this survey, "I have to satisfy myself." For all practical purposes, high-achieving interviewees were all concerned with excellence in their own performance, and all felt that their own personal standards transcended the norm.

## RISK TAKERS

These people also expressed a predilection for challenge, for experiencing new events, and described themselves as "risk-takers." Thus, they appeared to be oriented toward the future, to new possibilities and opportunities, and they seemed to relish the potential risks associated therein. Another piece of the puzzle was that they exuded boundless energy. They were quick in speech as well as in wit. They were dominated by an absorption in what they did and were concerned with demonstrating, mostly to themselves, that they could achieve consistently with their own high standards.

Narcissists are freer than other types; they don't listen to the usual social pressures to conform. Who wouldn't want freedom, or rather, who wouldn't want to chart their own course? But many people would rather have the security of a job, even a bad job, than have to come up with their own plan. However, narcissists can't stand situations that contain them and their ideas and they have the guts to go out on their own, risking both security and failure in favor of their vision.

It's no wonder that Sinatra couldn't have continued to be a band singer, even though leaving the band meant taking risks—but that was preferable to remaining in a situation that placed restrictive boundaries around him.

## INNER-DIRECTED STANDARDS

From interviews, Maehr (1986) concluded that high achievers are distinguished by self-reliance and goal-directedness. In short, they know what they want to do, and they believe they can rely heavily on themselves to accomplish it. Oddly enough, they do not exceed the rest in competitiveness. Maehr began to realize in his interviews that although competition with a standard of excellence was important, the standard ultimately is not externally based; rather, it is more internalized. The benchmark for high achievers becomes themselves. Just beating others is no longer primary; instead, consistency with their self-image is the standard to be achieved.

Budd Schulberg's famous novel, *What Makes Sammy Run?* describes the rise of a fictional show-business character from obscurity to fame, and those he had to step over to get there. It is tempting to pose the same question in Sinatra's case. But it is a difficult question to ponder. Sinatra's nature is too complex, too often contradictory, with apparently irreconcilable elements fused into the personality of the man and the legend. In the ultimate analysis, only Sinatra himself could say what makes him run.

## PERSEVERANCE

The person who has big dreams about themselves and the struggle to pursue them is bound to fail at one time or another. The way that a person reacts to failure is what differentiates the productive narcissist from the unproductive one. The productive ones are not discouraged by failure. They are resilient, they learn from it, rebound, and don't give up.

Sinatra's life is certainly a reflection of this, especially during the downturn that he faced before he was able to come back and win the Oscar for *From Here to Eternity*.

And that is where he found Angelo Maggio. In 1952, Sinatra read *From Here to Eternity*, James Jones' epic novel of pre-Pearl Harbor Army life, and recognized himself in a runt private who was nobody's patsy, who would sooner be beaten to death than ever give up. "I was Maggio," he would say. 'No matter who said what, I would prove it, no matter how many tests I was asked to make, no matter what the money, I was going to become Maggio if it was the last thing I ever did." (Kaplan, 2010) Columbia Pictures owned the rights, so he launched a campaign. He called studio chief and notorious bastard Harry Cohn, whom he knew well. "Harry," he said, "you've got something I want.:" Cohn replied, "What—you want to play God?" Frank begged, but Cohn could not see him as Maggio. "Look, Frank, that's an actor's part. You're nothing but a fucking hoofer." Frank was relentless, offered to work for nothing, sent Cohn a barrage of telegrams, signing each one "Maggio." He was in Africa with Ava when Cohn agreed to give him a screen test. Frank paid his own way back to Hollywood, improvised the bar scene where he threw the olives like dice, flew back to Africa, waited. Cohn capitulated. Frank, who had been making $150,000 per picture, would get $8,000 to play Maggio. And then the rest was history.

Burt Lancaster remarked, "His fervor, his anger, his bitterness had something to do with the character of Maggio, but also with what he had gone through in the last number of years: a sense of defeat, and the whole world crashing in on him, his marriage to Ava going to pieces . . . You knew this was a raging little man who was, at the same time, a good human being." (Kaplan, 2010)

## COMEBACK AND REINVENTING HIMSELF

Sinatra attained superstar status in the early 1940's as a young singer with the Tommy Dorsey band. But while his forties recordings with

Dorsey and later with the arranger Axel Stordahl are often very appealing, they show little of the depth, darkness and complexity he achieved in his fifties recordings. The transition from the forties to the fifties was very transformative. By the end of the forties his popularity was in freefall, his private life a shambles, and his voice a wreck. Sinatra's comeback in the early fifties, after being considered "washed up" by the press and Hollywood, is the stuff of showbiz legend. He divorces Nancy, marries Ava; record sales decline; fired by MGM, his voice fails through throat hemorrhages; he divorces Ava; attempts suicide; plays Maggio in *From Here to Eternity*, wins Oscar; moves from Columbia to Capitol Records; teams up with Nelson Riddle. What remains most remarkable about this episode in Sinatra's career is the completeness with which he reinvented himself in the fifties. Sinatra had a real genius for self-revision; much of his fascination as a cultural icon lies in the restless way he kept redefining himself for new audiences and new *Zeitgeists*. The boyhood crooner who thrilled the bobby soxers gave way to the tough, worldly, swinging lover, with hat cocked, cigarette dangling, and coat thrown over his shoulder. Sinatra's appeal in the forties lay not only in the sweetness of his voice but the vulnerability it conveyed. With his notoriously thin frame, his floppy bowtie, and drooping curls, he seemed exposed and helpless in the face of powerful feelings – his own and those of his fans. His songs of the period – "If You Are But a Dream," "I'll Never Smile Again," express adolescent longing, dreams of romantic love unhampered by experience. Yet if the swinger of the fifties seemed infinitely more jaded and knowing, invoking his inamorata not as "darling" but as "baby," and singing of love not as a romantic dream but as "The Tender Trap," Sinatra found subtle ways to keep the essential vulnerability of his younger persona in view.

Long after the headlines, the battles, and the passing myths that surround Sinatra have vanished, there will remain the hard, unalterable core of his work, on record and on film. That legacy is what the essential Frank Sinatra will come to mean – a unique voice that belongs to a unique legend.

His enduring appeal is *heart*, a term that, when applied to him, means many things. On the most obvious level, it refers to sentimental human emotion, and the musical rendering of that emotion begins and ends with Sinatra. "If the song is a lament at the loss of love," he has said, "I get an ache in my gut, I feel the loss myself and I cry out the loneliness, the hurt and the pain that I feel." No one was any better at wringing emotion from songs – not only sadness and loneliness, but also happiness, love, *joie de vivre*, and nostalgia – and folks kept coming back for more. His exhibitionism was connected with an increase in his self-esteem gained through the fact that others both looked at him and were excited by him.

## Impact

*Heart* also refers to Sinatra's courage. The reason that Sinatra's personal life continued to make news is that there are probably far more intense Sinatra lovers and Sinatra bashers than there are neutral parties, and he was the kind of person who seemed to believe that the measure of a person's character is sometimes best judged by the quality of his or her enemies. Those who hate him love the basher biographies and lurid press accounts; those who love him think all the better of him because of the bad press he gets. Interestingly, his fans often cite his great kindness to friends and strangers as evidence of his essential goodness, but they do not necessarily dismiss as untrue the accounts of his head-on-collisions with various individuals such as gossip columnists.

Pete Hamill once said that it would take "some combination of Balzac and Raymond Chandler" to capture the complexities of Frank Sinatra's life and work. Or, as Michiko Kakutani remarked: "It's an American story – a story that not only stars an artist of myriad complexities but also embodies immigrant dreams and Gatsbyesque ambitions, the rise of 20th-century American popular culture and the nervous relationship between entertainment and politics and the underworld."

Certainly more than other singers, he needed to make an impact on the way songs were to be sung and interpreted. And in this endeavor he became a dream force, a conveyor of our dreams, creating a fantasy of love, loss, pain, devotion and excitement. And then came the fall from grace, when his voice went, as did his celebrity status; and then the comeback.

His later albums explore every avenue of possibility: knowledge, reflection, friendship, travel, swinging in most of its manifestations, and finally, accomplishment and power. His greatness is his ability to lay bare the emotional facts. These albums are about continuing, and not only continuing, but trying to get better in spite of the realities of aging. They are heroic feats of self-generation, of finding more with less and gaining in the struggle a reason for going on.

## THIRST FOR LEARNING

Sinatra's later singing has a verve and conviction that make his records from the forties sound bland. He had learned to tease and twist a vocal line without violating its integrity. He learned to forward a song's rhythmic impetus by the percussive articulation of the one-syllable words – such as at the outset of the first song, "You Make Me Feel so Young," which suggests the association between youthful energy and his swinging idiom.

*Only the Lonely,* recorded in May and June 1958, may be his greatest album – the quintessential combination of deeply emotional songs, telling arrangements, youthful resources and interpretive maturity. The cover of the album tells a further story. The jacket comes adorned with a clown portrait of Sinatra's face, a maudlin touch reflecting his own predilection for clowns when he himself painted. His song selection on this album is nearly flawless: a sequence of brokenhearted torch songs that are never gratuitously depressing or unvarying in their gloom. They are wonderful songs from fine songwriters, either older masters of American popular music or younger men linked directly with Sinatra's circle. The songwriters that Sinatra drew around him were the best of their time, such as Cahn and Van Heusen, Burke, Mercer, and Arlen and Styne.

Many critics have noted the connection between the theme albums and various stages of Sinatra's personal life. It is not uncommon for artists to transmute the joys and pains of personal experience into their artistic accomplishments. This ability may not account totally for the emotional depth of their work. Sinatra's recordings appear to be personal statements even when they are tempered by the input of the composers, lyricists arrangers, band members, and recording company personnel with whom he worked.

Robin Douglas-Home (Jewell) describes a Sinatra recording session which, initially, he could see but not hear: "I saw complete and utter involvement with the song he was singing – involvement so close that one might feel he was in the throes of composing both tune and lyrics as he went along . . . He was putting so much into that song, giving off so much of himself that it drained my own energy just to watch him without hearing a note he was singing; it left me so limp that I felt I had actually been living through some serious emotional crisis." (1999, p. 83)

Frank would add, delete or abbreviate words and interject "hipsterism," alter the melody, adjust the cadence, slur from one note to the next or extend particular consonants and vowels, rearrange the sections of a tune, bite off a line, use growls or other guttural sounds, and intentionally strain his voice to convey a specific emotional state and create cadence.

Riddle mentions that when Frank got in front of an orchestra, the orchestra swung. Frank had authority, and he had incredible timing.

Bing Crosby, on the other hand was a crooner, but his renditions never intimated danger – they were always tuneful and pleasant. His public persona matched his music, and no one ever saw a dangerous side of Crosby. Sinatra's public persona has for years exuded danger. He has been described as generous, vulnerable, tender, loyal, hostile, surly, as well as dangerous.

Singers want to develop a style. They work at it, strive for it, and sometimes they contrive it. Sinatra instinctively had a style; he was born with it and continued to develop it. The beauty of Sinatra is that he is word-conscious and story-conscious, and that's why he's so great. He is a storyteller. He's sensitive – so automatically he's sensitive to his words, to the story they tell.

In 1975, Gay Talese was sent by *Esquire* magazine to Los Angeles to interview Sinatra. Although the meeting had been arranged with the singer's publicist, Talese wound up spending about five days in L.A. without ever speaking privately with Sinatra. In his article, Talese recounts his interviews with Sinatra's protective retinue and what he was able to observe from a distance. He describes a number of Sinatras. One is a man who seems to be somewhat detached from the scene, wherever he is. Another is a person of enormous kindness and generosity. But the same Sinatra can, within the same hour, explode in a towering rage of intolerance should a small thing be incorrectly done for him, Talese warns. He views Sinatra as a "wholly unpredictable man of many moods and great dimension, a man who responds instantaneously to instinct – suddenly, dramatically, wildly he responds, and nobody can predict what will follow."

During a radio interview in the 1980's, Sammy Cahn, a longtime associate, commented on what he saw as the basic elements of the Sinatra legend: his fame and notoriety, his musicianship, and his mysterious personality. Pointing out that the singer's fame has endured for more than fifty years, he noted that the *New York Times* rarely went for several weeks without at least mentioning the singer's name.

Cahn recalled an incident that took place while they were recording the title tune for the film *The Tender Trap*. Just as Sinatra approached the last few bars, he suddenly stopped, stormed out of the recording booth, and confronted Cahn. "Did you see how high the note is for the last 'love' in the song?" he shouted. "How can you expect me to hit such a high note?" Cahn calmly responded, "Because you're Frank Sinatra."

The singer stormed back to the booth, began the next take, and, when he came to the infamous note, hit it perfectly and with a vengeance while glaring furiously at Cahn. As for Sinatra's personality, Cahn, like many others, had a difficult time figuring it out. He maintained that there are three questions about Sinatra that no one could ever answer at any given moment: What is he like? Where is he now? Will he show up tonight? (Sinatra, F., 1963, in Playboy Interview. (Chicago: Playboy Press,1967, p. 7.)

## HIS EARLY LIFE

We see the beginnings of the Sinatra personality early on. He was an only child and he was spoiled. From the beginning, the only child had money. He had a charge account at a local department store and a wardrobe so fancy that his friends called him "Slacksey." He had a second- hand car at fifteen. And in the depths of the Depression, after dropping out of high school, he had the ultimate luxury: a job unloading trucks at the *Jersey Observer*.

But he had bigger dreams. As we mentioned, when he told his mother that he wanted to be a singer, she threw a shoe at him. Still, the only child got what he wanted; eventually his mother bought him a $65 portable public-address system, complete with loudspeaker and microphone. She thus gave him his musical instrument and his life.

She also gave him some of her values. At home, she dominated his father; in the streets, she dominated the neighborhood through the use of Democratic patronage.

From adolescence on, Sinatra understood patronage. He could give his friends clothes, passes to the Palisades Park, rides in his car, and in return they could give him friendship and loyalty. Power was all, and that insight lifted him above so many other talented performers of his generation. Vic Damone might have better pipes, Tony Bennett a more certain musical taste, but Sinatra had power. Looking back, it is easy to see how Frank's character evolved from his family. While Marty, Frank's father, was quiet, reflective and brooding, Dolly tended to be loud, impulsive and fiery. A strong-minded and spirited woman, Dolly usually prevailed in any heated discussion between the two of them. Marty was ambitious, but he was clearly more easygoing than Dolly.

Frank remembered that his father used to aid bootleggers. He was a tough guy and his job was to follow trucks with booze so that they weren't hijacked. He remembered when he was three or four that he heard sounds of crying and wailing. His father had gotten hit on the head and he came home bleeding all over the kitchen floor. His mother was hysterical and after that he got out of that kind of business and opened a saloon. They had a lot of shady friends because of the bar they ran. They owned a bar during Prohibition, so they would have had association with gangsters.

Someone who knew Dolly well remarked that as a woman of action, she supported her husband during the onset of his political career and ultimately he was elected mayor of Hoboken. She could speak with a longshoreman's vocabulary if necessary or be eloquent if she had to impress the political hierarchy in order to make a point.

Dolly was a model of unpredictable narcissism. "She had the roughest language of any female I've ever known," another friend remarked. "One time she walked into a party from pouring-down rain and the first thing she said when she got into the door was 'Holy Jesus! It's raining sweet peas and horseshit out there.'" She was the devil. Her mouth dripped with honey one minute and the next it was 'Fuck this' and 'Fuck that.'"

Frank's father also contributed to the often unexpected side of his son's character: his brooding pensiveness, his kindness, and his loyalty to friends. But his near-obsession with cleanliness, his unyielding stubbornness, and his legendary temper can be clearly traced to his mother. Sometimes young Frank would be so angry that his temper would simmer and then erupt and there would be nothing he could do about it.

From an early age, Sinatra had a petulant, spoiled streak that dictated that if he didn't get his way, not only did he not want to be in the game, he didn't even want to know the players. He was an only child in a culture and at a time when most people had large families. Children who have siblings usually learn about cooperation and sharing, about having to be reasonable. Not Frank. As an adult, he would always want it his way. If that wasn't possible, if he was crossed, he would simply disappear from the offender's life. "My son is just like me," Dolly once said in passing. "You cross him and he never forgets."

Even as an adolescent, Frank possessed ambition in his bones. It was an ambition formed at least in part by the then-dawning age of radio. As Frank told writer Pete Hamill, "The radio was like a religion. They were even shaped like cathedrals." On the stage he maintained an illusion of a personal connection to audience members that he had forged in his apprenticeship on radio.

Frank was about seventeen by the time he started singing with small bands in clubs on weekends and evenings. His mother helped him get bookings at Democratic Party meetings. He also performed at school dances. The more his parents and friends began to approve of his ambition, the more concrete Frank's plans became, until finally the idea of becoming a successful entertainer was a goal that he hoped to realize.

Early in his singing career, he discovered that the Sicilians owned the nightclubs and other venues that presented the kind of entertainment in which he was involved. These men were tough, successful and had unquestioned power. That appealed to the undersized singer with the skinny frame. He wanted success and power, and he wanted them badly.

On September 8, 1935, nineteen-year-old Frank Sinatra got his first big break when he auditioned to appear on the popular *Major Bowes and His Original Amateur Hours*. Bowes' NBC radio show was broadcast live from the Capitol Theater in New York. At the time of Frank's tryout, another act from Hoboken auditioned, a group calling themselves the Three Flashes. The idea came to Bowes to team Frank up with this other act from Hoboken and call them the Hoboken Four.

When the group performed the Bing Crosby-Mills Brothers hit "Shine" on the Bowes show, and they were an instant success. They generated a huge turnout of telephone calls voting for them. Sinatra's voice was already in place, but he had not had the opportunity to show it off. The group with Frank on lead would make several other appearances, and he did tour as a singer with the group. This was a great opportunity for him to hone his talents as a singer as well as a performer.

Frank worked with the group for about three months until the end of 1935, when the other three members began resenting all of the attention he was receiving from audiences. It was hard for Frank to hold himself back and blend in with the group. He couldn't help flirting with the women in the audience, winking at them, showing just a little more personality than the other fellows during performances.

When the tension among them intensified, he decided to leave the group. He had always hoped to go solo. When he left and returned to his parents' home, he was greeted by his father's strong disapproval of the decision he'd made to leave the Hoboken Four. Marty, his father, then lashed out at Frank and told him that he would never amount to anything and that he was a quitter. Frank responded by telling his father that he should be more supportive. Then Dolly piped in, "The two of you are driving me nuts. If Frankie wants to sing, Marty, Jesus Christ, let him sing, will ya!"

So Frank went on singing and in a few months became the solo singer at the Rustic Cabin, a roadhouse in nearby Bergen County in Englewood Cliffs, New Jersey, two miles north of the George Washington Bridge. By this time he had met a tough promoter, Hank Sanicola, who had taken on the unofficial job of managing Frank. Hank became a close friend, advisor, and promoter, and a pivotal force for Frank. He got him the job at the Rustic Cabin, where he also waited tables and sang with the house band, and they were broadcast on WNEW, a station heard throughout the tri-state area.

Previously, he almost didn't get the job because the bandleader didn't like him. When Frank told Dolly this she was a bit relieved, but then she heard him sobbing in his room and she realized for the first time how important the job was to him and why singing would be an integral part of his life. So she called the mayor of North Bergen, who was also president of the New Jersey Musicians' Union. She asked him if he could do something for her son, and he promised to intercede; Frank did get another opportunity to audition for the position and this time he was hired.

Later, Dolly was so anxious that her son make a good impression at the Rustic Cabin that she "papered" the place with friends. While at the Rustic Cabin, Frank would commute back and forth between Hoboken and New York just to keep his finger on the pulse of what was going on in the city's nightlife. He constantly watched other performers, and would get himself booked on every radio show whose producers would let him sing. He was so determined to make it, he spent some of his hard-earned money on a voice-and-diction coach who helped him lose his New Jersey accent.

In early 1937, his cousin Ray helped Frank get a job on a fifteen-minute NBC radio program–a regular spot for the young singer–for seventy cents a week. "He'd do anything he could," said another cousin. "It didn't matter where, when, or for how much. If he could sing, he'd sing. And by the time he was twenty-one, he was getting to be good."

By 1938, twenty-two-year-old Sinatra was having intimate relationships with any woman who seemed even the least bit willing. While he really was not good-looking, the women swarmed all over him whenever he got offstage after a performance. He'd tie them to the bed and make love to them and they let him do that. No one did that kind of stuff in the thirties—it was not part of the culture of lovemaking. Sex was constantly on his brain and he became very intense about it. He was extremely erotic, so sexy, and an intense kisser.

One woman recalled how he told her that he wanted to make passionate sex with her in a way that she would never, ever forget. "So c'mon, let Frankie in," he said as he unzipped her dress. "Let me love you baby, let Frankie in." In 1938, guys didn't talk like that. They didn't know how to romance a girl, but Frankie did. He was a cuddler, not a love'-em, leave-'em type. He'd stay the night, or at least slip out early in the morning, before her parents awakened. She felt loved, completely loved. She was thirteen, even though she looked, probably, eighteen.

There was talk about Frank's rather large penis. At first he was self-conscious about it, but then he started to appreciate its size and felt as if he were the biggest guy around. He got a certain respect, too, because of it. It gave him a stronger sense of manhood and it gave him an edge over the other guys who may have been more muscular, better-looking, or even more intelligent. They didn't have what he had, and while the size of his sex organ may have been a superficial matter to some, for Frank it worked. It gave him what he felt he needed: self-confidence.

Harry James was a well-known band leader who was auditioning singers in 1939. But when he heard Sinatra, he knew that he had a prize singer and Frank made his debut with the James Band soon afterward. James remarked to a reporter that Sinatra, "considers himself the greatest vocalist in the business. Get that! No one's ever heard of him. He's never had a hit record. He looks like a wet rag. But he says he is the greatest. If he hears you compliment him he'll demand a raise tonight."

When Tommy Dorsey heard Sinatra singing, he wanted to hire him to replace the band's vocalist, Jack Leonard. He offered Frank seventy-five dollars a week on a long-term contract. Of course, Frank wanted the job with a band that was well known and regarded. When he told James of the offer, James was understanding and just let him go, even though he didn't have to because there were seventeen months left on his contract.

"If Harry James instilled in Sinatra a greater feeling for jazz, Dorsey imparted to the young singer something more meaningful than his own prodigious technique: The concept of stating a melody so that it could instantly be recognized, yet at the same time personalizing it so that it sounded like a creation completely by or for the performer." (Friedwald, 1997)

Once with Dorsey, he recorded the song, "I'll Never Smile Again," and that record catapulted him to stardom and gave him top billing in the band.

Now Frank wanted to make his voice work in the same way that Dorsey played the trombone. He realized that in order to do this, to sustain those notes, he would need extraordinary breath control. So he began an intense swimming regimen in public pools, which he would find in cities on the tour. As he swam laps underwater, holding his breath, he would sing song lyrics in his head and approximate the time he would need to sustain certain notes. When he was back in Hoboken, he would continue his training by running on the track at the Stevens Institute of Technology. He would run one lap and trot the next, singing to himself, holding notes, practicing.

## SINATRA'S STYLE

Where other singers, at best, work with lyrics and melodies, Sinatra deals in mental images and pure feelings that he seems to summon up almost without the intervention of composers, arrangers, and musicians, as vital as their contributions are.

He completely revolutionized all of popular music before he turned thirty in 1945. He began the masterly synthesis of his earliest influences—the lyric-driven naturalistic approach of Crosby and the vulnerability and super-slow tempos of Billie Holiday— as expressed through the ultra-legato timing of mentor Tommy Dorsey. What Sinatra did was to psychologically communicate in his singing precisely what he was thinking at any given moment. After Sinatra, there was no longer any wall between performer and audience—he had invited listeners under his skin and into his heart. He perfected the art of intimacy, and that was a big contribution to popular music.

Sinatra doesn't simply embody certain clichés of maleness, he parodies them, and he does so precisely in order to allow a contrasting sense of the self's interior space to emerge.

It is important to recognize that Sinatra was not simply better than other popular singers of the fifties; he was fundamentally different from them, in ways that sometimes also hurt his career. His main rivals, Bing Crosby, Perry Como, Dean Martin and Nat Cole, all projected an easy, relaxed warmth that made them ideally suited to the casual intimacy of radio and television. Sinatra's first attempt at hosting a TV variety show flopped badly, and while he eventually made some successful specials, the medium never took to him as it did to Martin and Como. What he lacked was the kind of stable, identifiable stage personality that allows an audience to feel at ease in his presence. Sinatra's persona was too edgy, splintered, and ambiguous to translate to the small screen. Even in film, where he was quite prolific, he never developed a true star image. His true medium was the phonograph, especially the LP album, a form he virtually created in the fifties. The disjunctiveness of the form allowed him to explore a range of emotional tones, unfettered by the need to present a consistent persona. Treating each song as a discrete dramatic text, Sinatra gave himself to it with the same intensity and commitment a great actor brings to a role.

When we look closely at Sinatra's core repertoire of the fifties, certain themes emerge with obsessive frequency. Among these are the fragility of relations: songs like "I've Got the World on a String," "Wrap Your Troubles in Dreams," and "Get Happy" all express high spirits while glancing nervously over their shoulders. Another recurring theme is violence of love: in "All of Me" the singer methodically dismembers himself, inviting the lover to take his arms and lips, while in "I Get a Kick Out of You" he associates the sight of his beloved with a sharp blow to the posterior. A striking number of Sinatra's songs of this period are based on distinctions between age and youth: "Last Night When We Were Young," "You Make Me Feel So Young," "Young at Heart," "When the World Was Young." In all of these lyrics, age is a function of psychology more than chronology, and we're reminded again of Sinatra's existential shiftiness, his propensity for slipping from one state of being to another. Entering his forties in the mid-1950s, he is no longer embodied as a callow youth but hadn't yet earned the authority of age, and so his relation to those categories seems to waver with his self-image from song to song.

At the heart of his repertoire in this period is a group of songs that depict sexual desire as an invasive force, infiltrating body and mind and subjecting both to an insidious power often linked with rhythmic repetition. "Night and Day," "Day in, Day Out," "Old Devil Moon," "The Song Is You," and "Witchcraft" all ring variations on this motif, but the masterpiece of the group is undoubtedly Cole Porter's "I've Got You Under My Skin," widely considered to be Sinatra's single greatest recording.

## A Closer Look at His Style

At times, Sinatra seems to transform himself from tough guy to vulnerable man. The use of pause, hesitation, and delay to create a kind of musical experience is part of the secret here. If Sinatra's first impulse as a young singer was to master breath control so that he could produce long, continuous, legato lines free from artificial pauses, his second impulse was to learn where to put the pauses so that they could speak as forcefully as the words. The productive narcissist continues to learn and improve his performance. He is continually trying to reach higher potentials.

It was the level of his artistic intuition, combined with his careful attention to every last detail, that helped set Frank Sinatra apart from every other vocalist and make his recordings stand out as quintessential models, worthy of emulation.

To understand the significance of these performances, and how they fit into the overall scheme of what Sinatra, from early on, intended for his future, we must first consider the circumstances under which he created them. They were carefully planned and executed by an artisan who devoted a lifetime to perfecting his musical style, as well as to refining the craft of recording it for posterity.

It wasn't until he signed with Columbia Records in 1943 that Sinatra gained almost complete control over his sessions and focused on the elements that would aid him in realizing the perfection he sought. The Columbia years (1943-1952) find the singer experimenting with a wide variety of musical settings, laying a solid foundation for what (ten years later) would be his great period with Nelson Riddle, Billy May, and Gordon Jenkins. It was there that Sinatra became intimately acquainted with the most personal of creative processes and learned the value of keeping a watchful eye on the proceedings. Undoubtedly, a determining factor in the beauty of the recordings beginning around this time was the direct supervision of the singer himself. From the Columbia era on, Sinatra simply choreographed his own recording sessions, a task that most other artists, whether through feelings of supremacy or inadequacy, ignorance or apathy, left to those around them.

Sinatra assumed responsibility for and oversaw nearly every facet of his recording date from start to finish. Other singers would assign the work to different personnel. This attitude quickly turned his recording sessions into occasions that those who participated in remember as genuine "events" in every sense of the word. This was the aim of a classic productive narcissist.

George Avakian, the producer, talked about feeling intimidated by him. Frank would come off the elevator with his bodyguards. Two guards would come off the elevator first, and they'd look right and left. Then Frank would step out, and the two other guys stayed close to him. Once inside the recording studio, the atmosphere relaxed, and from all accounts, Sinatra became just another guy in the band or in the booth. Any air of superiority was left at the door, and for good reason. Sinatra simply knew that what went down in the studio was a permanent record and a reflection of his aesthetic values. He knew that his existence as a popular singer depended on the cooperation of many people, not the least of which were the musicians who helped make his songs "sing," and the technicians entrusted faithfully to preserve them.

Frank had respect for musicians and he knew everybody in the orchestra. Musicians agreed that he had a charisma that no one else did. This sentiment has been echoed by dozens of sidemen and technicians who have spent years working with him. Everything hinged on the fundamental basis for his work—the song. Beginning with the right tune was always of primary importance, an essential ingredient in Frank's recipe for success. When, in the mid-1980s, Sinatra felt that he had exhausted the ubiquitous supply of standard songs, he implored young songwriters to write better music. "There's nobody writing good songs anymore," he often lamented. "I wish some new cat would come along and write something decent for me."

When recording, and considering tunes that would become part of an album, Sinatra himself would sit down and make the selections, then work out the order of the program, carefully controlling the pacing and flow of what he envisioned for the final record. Here is what he says about this:

> "First, I decide on the mood for an album, and perhaps pick a title. Or sometimes it might be that I have the title, and then pick the mood to fit it. But it's important that there should be a strong creative idea for the whole package. Like *Only the Lonely* or *No One Cares,* for instance. Then, I get a short list of maybe sixty possible songs, and out of these, I pick twelve to record. Next comes the packing of the album, which is vitally important. I put the titles of the songs on twelve bits of paper, and juggle them around like a jigsaw puzzle until the album is telling a complete story, lyric-wise. For example, the album is in the mood of "No One Cares" – track one. Why does no one care? Because there's "A Cottage for Sale," track two. And so on until the last track . . . the end of the episode." (Douglas-Home p. 36.)

Arguably, Sinatra was at his finest during 1953-1962, reaching the absolute peak of vocal perfection in early 1955, as evinced by the incredibly supple intonation and vocal shading he achieved on the classic album *In the Wee Small Hours.* In addition to his voice's maturing to a naturally darker tone, it was around this time that he began to take more noticeable liberties with the timing and meter of his vocal lines, within the context of the musical orchestration.

In a radio interview, Sinatra talked about the importance of looking at the lyric and understanding it, finding out where you want to accent something, where you want to use a soft tone. His 1956 versions of "Night and Day" and "From This Moment On," reveal awesomely powerful, subliminally sexual overtones, stunningly achieved through the mounting tension and release of the musical arrangement and Sinatra's beat-teasing vocal lines. He knew what was going to be important. It took twenty-two takes to reach a level of perfection that satisfied him for Cole Porter's "I've Got You Under My Skin," the impeccable reading confidently affirming the validity of his artistic rebirth, forever etching

Sinatra, vintage 1956, into the American consciousness. Sublimely erotic and seductive, this recording is surely the turning point in the Sinatra-Riddle period, the pivot upon which all future Sinatra efforts would hinge.

When he hears a particularly sensitive passage, he cocks his head, leans in, and shrugs his shoulder. With a knowing smile, he nods appreciatively to Gordon Jenkins. One thing is clear: Sinatra invests as much of his soul in grooving on a playback as he does in the actual performance. It shows here in this rare glimpse of Sinatra digging Sinatra!

"Reading a lyric" not only entails giving each word its appropriate emotional nuance, but also conveying the dramatic situation and assuming the character – the "persona" – conjured up by the words of the song.

Sinatra's album *The Voice* is thought to be the first "concept" album. No singer before him – not even Bing Crosby – understood the potential of a record album as something more, that the tunes could relate to one another and be sequenced in a way that would tell a complete, emotional story, as did the songs in *The Voice*. It could take weeks of planning and progress song by song. But he felt that it was worth it. He had the final say over the songs that would be included in the album. Once in the studio, Sinatra always took his recording sessions seriously. Unlike many artists who haphazardly recorded vocals at a producer's or arranger's direction and then anxiously awaited the song's release, Sinatra was involved in some way, even if unofficially, in nearly every aspect of the session, from the choosing of musicians to the fine-tuning of the arrangements.

It's startling to note just how busy and productive Frank Sinatra was in the middle of the 1950's. with both memorable record albums and noteworthy movies. By this time, it was estimated he was making about $4 million a year. Considering his schedule, it was amazing that he found the time to host his own television series of big-budgeted one-hour musicals and half-hour dramas for ABC-TV, *The Frank Sinatra Show*, aired in 1957. In that year, he recorded an astonishing fifty-seven new songs, but probably none are more significant than "Witchcraft" and "All the Way." This was also the year of Frank's classic concept albums, *A Swingin' Affair* and *Come Fly With Me*, which would soar to number one on the sales charts. His output was amazing: four or five, sometimes more, albums a year.

After his "down" period, the honors soon returned to him again. He was at the top of *Down Beat's* best male vocalist poll in 1955 after seven years of exile; singer of the year with *Metronome;* No.1 singer and best album-maker (*Swing Easy*); and best single (*Young At Heart*) with the critics who cast their votes in *Billboard*. These events were the precursor to six years of most intense activity, during which Sinatra would record his great albums, star in seventeen films, including the best he ever made, and roar around doing concerts and club dates with girlfriends and his gang of male associates, continually making headlines as the carefree, exuberant adult swinger. The key to his existence now was that he became essentially his own boss. He had achieved a complex agglomeration of private companies which controlled him as he controlled them. In the words of Mitch Miller, "He had a direction. He knew where he was going, come hell or high water." (Friedwald, 1997)

## HIS EXHIBITIONISM

Beyond talent, beyond technique, the palpable but invisible power of every great star stems from the need to be seen and to be held in the imagination of the audience. This is a particular kind of narcissism, in that he becomes the center of attention and captures the attention of the audience. Sinatra's singing in this period was more than a sound; it was an attitude. He gave us words, postures, rhythms—a sense that sex and life were going to be a big "wowie."

When times began to change, he had to stay fresh, trying *bossa nova* with the Brazilian Antonio Carlos Jobime and mining the jazz scene in collaborations with Duke Ellington and Count Basie, which led to his touring with the Basie band and recording three albums with Basie, including the thrilling live album *Sinatra at the Sands*.

The word "control" is central to attempting to understand the highly complex and enigmatic personality of Frank Sinatra. Even when he first started working on New York radio stations and in North Jersey roadhouses in the late 1930's, he knew he possessed an undeniable talent for singing popular music. In the years in which Sinatra's singing style was perfected, his diction and his ability to convey the innate meaning of lyrics enabled him to become better and better.

"Sinatra learned to create a new character with each song. He shifts from attitude to attitude with every new text the way singers normally use different keys for each tune. Although he's always warm and tender and vulnerable, it's the gradations of and variations on these qualities that make him, in Wodehouse's words, 'One of the godlike kind of men.'" (Friendwald, 1997, p. 153)

Obviously, his perception of himself must have been someone who was volatile, daring, and full of adventure. This is not someone who ambles through life, but rather speeds through much like a racing car going more than 200 mph.

Throughout his life, Sinatra relished being in the company of "wise guys," enjoying having their aura of power rub off on him. Similarly, they were extremely loyal to him, and over the years he continued to maintain his obligations to them. When things turned especially bad for him in 1951 and 1952, these powerful men kept his career alive.

Margaret Whiting, who had frequent access to the Sinatra/Riddle recording sessions, recalled, "Sometimes Frank would come in the studio, and he was looking at his watch as if to say, 'C'mon, c'mon, let's get going.' He had a girl to see, or he was going somewhere... Other times he was fascinated about an arrangement, and he would do it over and over. He'd say, 'Play it slower, play it softer,' and he would really get a record out of it. He loved the arrangements. Other times he was bored to tears and wanted to get out of there." One time Sinatra had insisted on doing twenty-eight takes of the tune "Rain," which immediately preceded the recording of "Young at Heart."

Nelson Riddle said that he was only afraid of one man, and that was Frank Sinatra. "Not physically. He was afraid of him because he couldn't figure out what he would do . . . which is why Nelson wanted a first reading every time we played. He wanted it perfect the first time so as not to give Frank a chance to not like the chart."

Once Nelson's son, Chris, suffered a broken pelvis after being hit by a car while delivering newspapers. Nelson learned of the accident right in the middle of a record date. "Frank went into the booth and called three specialists and said, 'Get to Santa Monica Hospital right now and do what you need to do to save his life.' He took care of everything. That was really something, to see Frank really take charge and get those people out there—boom, boom—and then we finished the date."

Within two years of the 1953 release of *From Here to Eternity*, Sinatra had disproved of the judgment of the pundits. He had transformed himself into the most powerful force in Hollywood as an actor, recording star, and nightclub attraction. His enigmatic, chameleon-like ways, however, were often infuriating to those he worked with; he once admitted that he was his own worst enemy.

If his concern for his recordings and his attention to detail moved him up on the ladder to success, his relation to his acting career followed a similar path. The productive narcissist needed to continue to climb the ladder of success. In fact, at a Yale lecture he told the journalist Sidney Zion that he kept thinking to himself, "I've got to climb a little higher in this next year. What could I do in six months? How far could I go?"

Through sheer force of talent and willpower, he had fulfilled his dream of movie stardom, won Hollywood's top honor, and reminded everyone in Filmland that he had arrived as a top-flight dramatic actor. There were no longer light comedic roles or parts as a song-and-dance man opposite Gene Kelly—no, he was a dramatic force in Hollywood. What he was able to do with his singing, his varied moods and interpretation of lyrics, he now invested in the varied roles that he was to play.

He had the depth and range in acting every bit the equal of his work in the recording studio. More than that, he invoked a similar interest in the roles that he played as he did in the albums he made. This attempt at plumbing the darkness of his roles didn't interest other singing actors like Bing Crosby. However, Bobby Darin seemed to follow very much in the mold of Sinatra. Sinatra did have a serious competitor in Marlon Brando, and even though he outhustled and outbid Brando for the rights to *The Man With the Golden Arm*, his lack of training as an actor may have kept him from reaching the heights of a Brando. On the other hand, this could be said of most other actors whether they had training or not. Brando was so unique and extraordinary, that it would be unfair to compare Sinatra to him.

> When Sinatra realized that he could have a movie career, he didn't just wing it. In fact he visited sets, observed directors, and studied the actors. It's not just that Sinatra wanted to succeed. He *had* to succeed. "I went around to all the different sets in the studio, and watched the different people work, all the veterans. I'd stand up on a ladder way in the back and pick up pointers from these people. I still have never had a dramatic coach. I suppose I should have. I almost regret that I didn't." He went on to describe his attitude toward acting. "I always try to remember three things as a movie actor. First, you must know *why* you are in the movie, understand all the reactions of the man you are playing, figure out *why* he's doing what he is doing. Secondly, you must know the script . . . I keep a script in my office, my car, my bedroom, by the telephone, even in the john. And I read the whole script maybe fifty or sixty times before shooting even starts . . . Thirdly, you must learn and listen to the lines of others; it's no good just learning your own . . . I have my own technique that I've evolved from discussing acting with some of my chums, like Spencer Tracy and Bogie when he was alive . . . Once we've begun shooting I rarely open the script. If two good actors in a scene listen intently to what the other is saying, they'll answer each other intelligently. Actors who go only by the lines never seem to be listening to the other actor, so the scene comes out on the screen as if you can see the wheels going around in their heads...Although movies were a crapshoot compared to music, where Mr. S. was undisputedly *numero uno*, cinema was the Everest Frank Sinatra felt compelled to conquer . . . Some dreams, like movie stardom, were beyond the bottom line. (Santopietro, 2008)

There were so many contradictory facets of his life: for example, his ex-wife Mia Farrow perceptively observed: "They have it all wrong, they don't really know him. They can't see the wounding tenderness that even he can't bear to acknowledge—except when he sings. Maybe if they look at the earliest photos of Frank . . . if they really looked at that face, almost feminine in its beauty, they'd see exactly who it was the Frank Sinatra the tough guy has spent his life trying to protect." Underneath all that brash behavior, away from the fun-filled nightclub gigs and the center-of-the-action persona he projected around the globe, life was never easy for Sinatra, or at least never easy for extended periods of time. In Frank's own highly self-aware words: "Nothing anybody's said or written about me ever bothers me—except when it does."

## SEX AND EMOTION IN HIS MUSIC

Frank Sinatra seduced an audience, both consciously and unconsciously, combining sex and overwhelming feelings of emotion with romance and compassion. In his personal life, Sinatra required the love of one utterly devoted woman, but professionally he seemed to need the love of the entire world. In the screaming bobby-soxers he nearly found the whole world, because word of the Sinatra hysteria soon spread around the globe. And if it was good enough for girls in New York, well, then, it became good enough for girls everywhere. "Sinatramania" was born. Bobby-soxers screamed because Frank injected sex into the music.

No wonder Sinatra loved F. Scott Fitzgerald's *The Great Gatsby*. It wasn't just that he and Jay Gatsby shared a fevered self-invention; it's that, like Gatsby, underneath the tough-guy exterior Frank always maintained his sense of wonder, and audiences responded to the tender-and-tough dichotomy.

He was a natural personality. No matter what he played, he was always Frank Sinatra, just as Clark Gable and Spencer Tracy were always themselves. His secret was complete concentration on what he was doing. There were no heights he couldn't reach, and not much he couldn't do if he put his mind to it.

When he was seventy-five years old, he gave sixty-five concerts in 1990, seventy-three in 1991, and eighty-four in 1992, hopping the globe to seventeen different countries as far away as Australia and Japan. (Contrast this with Barbra Streisand's first-ever European tour in 2007 at age sixty-five, a tour that consisted of fewer than twenty-five concerts).

Sinatra's life began and remained a fight to the finish; a fight against prejudice, expectations, and limitations imposed by others, a fight against loneliness and mortality. In this light, it makes perfect sense that Sinatra's last words to his wife Barbara were, "I'm losing." The official cause of death, a heart attack, was true enough, but the real cause was the inevitable collapse of his body after a lifetime of drinking and smoking, of late nights and little sleep, a collapse that was seemingly the only limitation Sinatra could never outrun, the only fight he could not continue.

At the time of his death, the director Martin Scorsese affirmed, "He was an idol of mine and of millions. A great Italian-American, a great American—and a great actor by the way—a great, great actor just alone in films like *Some Came Running* and *The Man With the Golden Arm* and *From Here to Eternity* . . . There will never be another him. You, know, he's the idol. He was the original."

Katharine Hepburn said that Sinatra was the greatest male pop singer in the history of America. "He had evolved from a pleasant lightweight performer on film to the most versatile male presence in movies, equally at home in a first-class musical such as *On the Town* or in the heaviest of dramas, like *The Man with the Golden Arm*." In his seventy-one film appearances, Frank Sinatra crafted a body of work unparalelled in American film history in its versatility. No other actor in Hollywood history had ever ranged so widely and so believably over such a long period of time. He may have made quite a few movies of little or no discernible merit, but as director George Sidney flatly declared: "There were no heights he couldn't reach."

CHAPTER FOUR

# The Ultimate Gamesman

Sinatra saw the entertainment business as inspired by the spirit of a game. Seeing it as a game, he knew the importance of getting the best team of people behind him and infused his performances with a fierce driven interest to win in this complicated contest.

The modern gamesman is best defined as a person who loves change as well as influencing its course. He sees human relations, as well as his career, in terms of options and possibilities. His character can be seen as a collection of contradictions. While he can be cooperative, he is also quite competitive; at other times he can be seen as detached and playful but compulsively driven to succeed; a team player, but a would-be superstar; a team leader, but often a rebel against bureaucratic hierarchy; fair and unprejudiced, but contemptuous of weakness; tough and dominating, but not destructive. The gamesman is energized to compete for the exhilaration of running his team and gaining victories. His main goal is to be known as a winner and his deepest fear is to be labeled a loser.

The entertainment business is a highly competitive industry that is run by cool and daring gamesmen. The stakes are high and there is fierce competition and pressure to accrue profits and remain on top. A spirit of intense struggle for the high rewards pervades the whole industry.

The successful people who play in this arena are a special breed of gamesmen who crave excitement, and if there is not enough of it at work they will gamble huge amounts of money. Sinatra was known to lose thousands of dollars at the gaming table. His ability to dramatize ideas and to stimulate others were among his most important assets. He constantly worked to win in the entertainment business. He could be seen as an imaginative gamesman who tended to create a new reality, less limiting than the normal everyday reality. Like many adolescents, he seemed to crave a more romantic, fast-paced, semi-fantasy life that could put him in danger of losing touch with reality; but he was able to keep this need under control and to distinguish between the game and the real world.

Since parts of him functioned as a gifted gamesman, he imagined himself in an incredible, romantic fantasy. He never traveled without an entourage. At his worst moments, he could be unrealistic, manipulative, and a compulsive workaholic. His hyped-up activity may have hidden doubts about who he was and where he was going. When he was let down, he was faced with feelings that made him feel powerless. The most compulsive players must be "turned on," energized, by competitive pressures. Deprived of a challenge, he could become bored and slightly depressed. Life was meaningless outside the game. He was able to keep the energy turned on by his compulsive drinking, which fueled his vigor in life. However, he had a keen ability to size up the game before him and then take charge of the situation. He felt as if he were a cowboy entering a city or village alone on his horse, and of course packing a pistol.

Magic Johnson was a basketball player unto himself, and a really great point guard. He was able to see the whole court and make things happen in a blink. He knew where everyone was on the court, and he was able to size up positions very quickly. He was an incredible passer and a great team leader and player, even as a rookie. He was the kind of player who made his teammates better, and you could tell how much they loved playing with him. Magic loved getting his teammates involved in the flow of the game, and he had a unique touch in the way he approached it. Fellow teammates would say that out of all the players, if they wanted to give the ball to somebody to make a play, they would vote to give it to Magic. He could play inside and outside, any position, and make it work for his team.

Magic was a facilitator, and he had a special gift that would bring excitement into the game. He was able to run the fast break as well as anyone in the history of the game, and that's why he is thought of as a dominant player who would shine in any era. He certainly stood out among the point guards in the game.

A point guard in basketball is given the task of organizing the plays that have been planned before the game. He must have a total picture of how the players will mesh and contribute to the team's victory. That's why point guards are one of the most essential parts of the game. They must be able to handle the ball, pass, and run the court in a flash. They need a particular attitude and courage to pull the players together and make their team stronger.

It is in this context that I refer to Sinatra as the dazzling "point guard," or, in other words, the ultimate gamesman. The gamesman's main interest is in challenge and competitive activity, where he can show that he will come out on top. In short, he responds to work and life as if it's a game. The contest hypes him up and he communicates his enthusiasm to others, thus energizing them. He enjoys new ideas, new techniques, and fresh approaches. His talk and his thinking are terse, dynamic, sometimes playful, and they come in quick flashes. His main goal in life is to be a winner, and talking about himself invariably leads to a discussion and strategy about what a player he will be in the showbiz contest.

Sinatra was constantly in pursuit of new ideas and approaches to music, and therefore his albums evolved in very creative ways. He was very good at facilitating a team. He brought into play a team spirit; he was the leader, and the number two person was the orchestrator, Nelson Riddle; then came the composer, Jimmy Van Heusen and the lyricist, Sammy Cahn, and finally the promoter, George Evans. They became a winning team that enabled Sinatra to stand out far ahead of the other crooners of the day.

Since he was responding to life as a game, inventiveness, flexibility, and the love of novelty were driving forces in Sinatra's evolution. He liked to take calculated risks and was fascinated by creative techniques and new ways of staying on top.

Sinatra was not bigoted and as a liberal he believed that everybody who is good should be allowed to play, and that race, sex, religion, or anything else had no bearing, except for contributing to the team. While he took no pleasure in another man's defeat, that did not imply that he was sensitive to others' feelings or sympathetic to their special needs. However, at times he could be quite compassionate and was generally fair and usually open to new ideas. In fact being open to new ideas is what kept Sinatra in the public eye throughout his career.

I use the term "game" to imply finding the things that you love to do and then making sure that you do them well. These have been called magical feeling states. What are these magical states? For a moment, let's take a look at artists in their creativity. The artist has an intense feeling of interest and excitement during the act of creating. It provides a tremendous exhilaration, though we know that there are other fields that can provide similar pleasures. The artist is enthralled by the pleasure of creating—a drive within him that fosters a feeling of unbelievable magnitude.

Since Sinatra was so concerned about winning and turning out top recordings, he evaluated the other players almost exclusively in terms of what they could do for the team. He was ready to replace a player as soon as he felt that person weakened the performance. Often his strengths resembled those of an adolescent, in that he was playful, industrious, fair, enthusiastic, and open to new ideas. Yet he also had the adolescent's yearning for independence and ideals while needing to maintain an illusion of limitless options, which restricted his capacity for personal intimacy.

One facet of Sinatra's life that could have been more destructive for him than it was, was his fascination with hoodlums and Mafia associates—but even they became part of the game.

The major danger and pitfall is that at their worst moments, gamesmen like Sinatra are unrealistic, manipulative, and compulsive workaholics. Their hyped-up activity conceals doubt about who they are and where they are going. Their ability to escape from reality allows them to avoid unpleasant experiences. The most compulsive players must be "turned on," energized by competitive pressures. Life loses a lot of meaning outside the game and they tend to create activities that will lessen their boredom. But once the game is on, as in a recording schedule, making a film, or preparing for a concert with deadlines they must meet, they come to life, become serious, and in turn are very productive.

The gamesman's yearnings for autonomy and fear of being controlled contribute to a common mid-career uneasiness. Impatient with red tape and unwilling to be boxed in, some try to skirt authority, as in Sinatra's case when he felt compelled to start his own record company.

Bedazzled by the perpetually adolescent charm of the gamesman and sympathetic to their struggles to achieve, our society romanticizes them. One might say that although we have few heroes because we have lost faith in our leaders, the gamesman is our favorite anti-hero. The fatal danger for the gamesman is to be trapped in perpetual adolescence, never outgrowing the self-centered compulsion to score, never confronting the deep boredom with life when it is not a game, never developing a sense of meaning that requires more of them and allows others to trust them.

Sinatra was in a continual quest for excitement and was turned on by constantly venturing into different territories. He couldn't stop performing or acting in 65 movies—good ones, bad ones, it almost didn't matter—what mattered was the game itself, which meant he was always working and having fun, and of course his winning was measured by the vast amounts of money he was both making and spending.

He took Vegas by storm, and even owned a piece of the Sands Hotel. This was the game of control and ownership. His presence led to sold-out performances, since his public couldn't get enough of him. His friendship with the Mafia, who were the tough guys, became the game of power. You are as important as whom you know and hang out with as well as who is afraid of you. And Sinatra only gravitated to important and significant people, from presidents to gangsters, which makes this also a particular kind of game. And he slept with the most desirable and gorgeous women in Hollywood—Lana Turner, Marilyn Maxell, and Marilyn Monroe. And we could call this the seduction game.

He knew instinctively how to play the different games of life. He functioned much like a coach of baseball, basketball or football. You have to get the best players and then adopt the most effective strategies and plays. These coaches can look at a team and grasp immediately the formula for success or unfortunately, failure. Of course, they need the talent to take them to the top, but they know the rudiments of the game and than spot talent very quickly.

Sinatra came to Hollywood, managed to get invited to the best parties, and then he took over and organized the parties and took command of who got invited. He becomes the chief honcho and it became his New Year's Eve party, as well as his entourage who got together after his shows. He was the orchestrator and, in short, it was Sinatra's world, or as the saying goes, "We just live in it."

Ultimately he was the gamesman who knew how the game should be played and then played it better than anyone else. But it was a very complicated game, and other singers could not possibly match his ability at becoming the point guard as well as his intense quest to reach the top of the mountain leading to success.

When Phil Jackson was hired to be part of the coaching staff of the Chicago Bulls in 1987, he wanted to find a structure that would empower everybody on the team and produce the best results possible. He pursued winners and won six NBA championships. Magic Jackson built one of the greatest teams in the history of the NBA, and they were consistent winners. His ability lay in melding his team and getting players to give up their usual "me-first" playing attitude—essentially, to pass the ball to the best players and let them run with it, and develop an offensive system that gave everybody on the floor a chance. He was able to see the game in a new and exciting way while bringing each player into his system.

Now let's compare this style to Sinatra's methods. When he decided to make it as a solo artist, he immediately hired the best arranger and built a team around the most gifted songwriters. He understood right from the beginning the importance of gathering around him the best team he could, one of the reasons he hired Bill Miller as his pianist. More than most singers he understood that a well-constructed team would enable him to be prominent year after year, in the same way Tommy Dorsey or Benny Goodman hired the best musicians for their orchestras and took on the most competent arrangers to keep their music progressing. Bands that did not keep strengthening their team often went out of business. And singers who did not continue to build a strong team of players often lagged in their later years. However, it was Sinatra who knew immediately what he needed in order to progress in the world of music.

Maccoby (1976) recounts a conversation he overheard involving a highly successful CEO who was at the top of his game. The CEO was recounting the many projects with which he was involved. A colleague, quite impressed if not overwhelmed, replied, "Wow, no rest for the weary." The CEO looked at him and said, absolutely straightfaced, "Why would you ever rest from what you love?"

The one man who from the very beginning sensed his true worth and potential was Frank Sinatra himself. Harry James back in 1939, years before Sinatra's success, told a *Down Beat* staffer: "He considers himself the greatest vocalist in the business." In a *New Yorker* profile in 1946, E. J. Kahn noted that Sinatra regarded his voice as an instrument without equal, and when other singers came up in conversation, he replied that "I can sing that son of a bitch off the stage any day in the week."

## Artistry

The popular singer is concerned with singing in a way that is intelligible, casual, and based on conversational phrasing. These goals take precedence over the soaring melodic heights achieved in opera. This kind of phrasing may not be easy to achieve. Some singers appear not to have a clue as to how to phrase a lyric. Music lovers often cringe at Vic Damone's stylistic deficiencies while lauding his lovely voice. But what does it serve to have vocal talent if it is not combined with successful lyric interpretation?

There are several Sinatras. Perhaps this is what makes him both fascinating and controversial. He was tempestuous, tender, searching, indefatigable, unexpected. As a father, he was doting, generous, always involved. He was overheard to remark to his daughter on the phone one day, "Yes, Nancy, go ahead, cut your hair if you feel you'll like it." He hung up, shaking his head slightly. "You know, Rosie, I never really left home," he said. He continued to make his family part of his team. Each daughter wrote a book about their father; his son became his orchestra leader and throughout his life his family was part of his team, showing up at his concerts and the parties he threw.

Then there is the other side. The story goes that after a performance Sinatra, still wound up, took a few pals to his favorite club, Jilly's South, where the go-go girls gyrated on five platforms until morning. "I don't go for topless," Sinatra says, "I've never seen a girl in a topless bathing suit, but I don't have to see one to know I wouldn't like it. I don't go for extreme cleavage, either. I like women to be women." He could never sleep before four or five A.M. When there was no one to drink or talk with, he read two to five newspapers daily, and ten magazines and five books per week. His interests were wide-ranging, his tastes catholic. He listened a lot, but when he started to talk, everybody else stopped.

## Rat Pack

In 1963 Frank Sinatra was at the height of his fame, the undisputed king of popular music and Hollywood. He was also the leader of the pack—the rat pack, the clan. The clan was really a gang for grownups that the late Humphrey Bogart invented one boozy night in 1955. He christened his gathering of renegades The Holmby Hills Rat Pack in 1955. Its purpose was drinking, whoring, and outraging any and all straight citizens. In real life, Bogart had been eerily similar to the thugs, gangsters, adventurers and private eyes he portrayed on the screen, and he attracted his middle-aged gang easily, naturally, and with very little hype.

After Bogie's death, the Rat Pack dissolved, to be reborn as Sinatra's clan. In the beginning, it was just a gang of hangers-on, exactly like the pack. It included Joey Bishop, the comic from South Philadelphia; Sammy Davis Jr., the black mascot; Dean Martin, an Italian crooner; Peter Lawford, the brother-in-law of JFK; and later other associate and affiliate members, like Milton Berle, Shirley MacLaine, and Tony Curtis.

Whatever the clan was, by 1963 it had become the most powerful single syndicate in Hollywood. Agents, producers, directors, writers,

## The Ultimate Gamesman

actors, actresses, and financial investors reacted to the clan's every whim. The performers the clan took under its protective wing prospered; those it dismissed as beneath contempt as squares and "clydes" found themselves effectively shut out of the entertainment world. When the clan was on the road in Vegas, New York, Atlantic City, Chicago, Philadelphia, Baltimore or any of the other whistlestops in between, the locus of power in Hollywood traveled with it. The clan made Joey Bishop's reputation. It damn near destroyed Eddie Fisher by showing up at his openings, heckling the performer good-naturedly, and actually taking over the stage. When Sinatra was in a good mood, the clan seemed warm, generous, philanthropic, but when Sinatra's lips narrowed and that charming smile dissolved into a frown, the clan could turn as vicious, vindictive and unforgiving as any other gang.

But it was this aura of adolescent charm that made headlines out of the Rat Pack. Frank and Dean Martin used to puncture tiny pinholes into the filters of friend's cigarettes so they wouldn't draw, or snip into their bow ties so that when they went to put them on the ties would fall apart in their hands. Cherry bombs were another favorite; those red-colored party explosives were thrown into yards, used to blow up mailboxes, tossed as ammunition against journalists, or set off at the end of someone's bed. Frank and Dean had a brown terrycloth robe made for Sammy Davis, Jr. at the Vegas steam room where they wore white robes, the same place where they shoved a naked Don Rickles out of the steam room door into the crowded pool area. Frank, a man who never slept on planes, regularly stuffed candy into the slipped-off shoes of those foolish enough to nod off.

With all the fun they had, sometimes the fun got to be a bit brutal. There is a comedian, Jackie Mason, who lives near me and often I encounter him while walking across 57th Street. I recently asked him about Sinatra, and he was more than willing to tell me about one particular incident. "I was performing in Vegas and Sinatra and a few guys came in and sat down. While I was trying to get a few jokes across to the audience, these guys started heckling me and interrupted my act. I looked at them and called Frank some name alluding to him being a "middle-aged juvenile delinquent." Some time after the show I left to go to my car. Someone caught up to me and punched me in the mouth, breaking my nose. And then I was threatened that much worse could happen to those who crossed Frank Sinatra."

Jackie then shook his head and said, "You had to be careful with those guys, they could really do you in."

## TOUGHNESS

As Sinatra became more successful, certain character traits emerged more intensely. He became a tough guy with the intent of inducing fear in others. He had an aura of power and of being right. This could be seen as strength of character, a winning attitude that creates fear in others. Most people backed off from it as if there were an aura of inner violence in Frank that could always explode.

It is difficult to know whether Sinatra sensed that it was necessary to be tough to keep himself on top, or whether the toughness was a self-protective mechanism that reassured him that he was not being taken advantage of or humiliated. His toughness acted to keep him out front and ahead of others. He knew that he could dominate each encounter and he wanted it that way. So his toughness might really have come from his courage to act on his instincts, unlike those who never really take a position. Throughout Sinatra's life, he took stands that others backed away from.

Certainly, prejudice was one issue that he always faced head on. In fact, his recording of the "House I Live In" was an early indication of how emotionally charged he could be when faced with any kind of prejudice.

The screenwriter who wrote the "House I Live In" was Albert Maltz, who was a card-carrying member of the American Communist Party. Later Maltz was brought before the House Un-American Activities Committee and cited for contempt of Congress for refusing to name names. Then he was imprisoned and, when released, he moved to Mexico.

About this time, Sinatra decided to produce a movie based on the story of *The Execution of Private Slovik,* who was the only U.S. soldier executed for desertion during World War II. Albert Maltz seemed the perfect choice to write the antiwar picture, however he had been blacklisted and no studio would hire him or distribute a film he had worked on.

This decision to hire Maltz was going to be one big problem for Sinatra, who was campaigning for John Kennedy, and Kennedy's staff knew that it would be a mistake to have Sinatra (left-leaning liberal) connected to Kennedy especially when he was running in the primaries.

When Sinatra announced that he had hired Maltz, he faced an avalanche of criticism. Murray Schumach from *The New York Times* asked Sinatra if he were fearful of the reaction in Hollywood, because he was openly defying the blacklist. Sinatra told him, "We'll find that out later and we'll see what happens."

And it didn't take long for him to find out what would happen. Prominent Hollywood stars such as Robert Taylor, Ward Bond, and John Wayne rushed to attack the decision. Editorial pages around America laid into Sinatra. Hedda Hopper joined the chorus and blasted Frank for hiring a Communist. However, Frank stood by his decision and said that he wasn't worried, because his records were selling better than ever and his concerts still packed in the audiences.

Hopper went on to call for a commercial boycott of Sinatra and General Motors threatened to pull its ads from three forthcoming Sinatra specials unless the singer dissociated himself from Maltz. When his lawyers flew to Palm Springs to try to dissuade him he said, "Fuck em, there will be other specials."

Finally, JFK's father, Joe Kennedy, called Frank and told him how upset they were with the decision to hire Maltz. And then he said, "It's either Maltz or us. Make up your mind." As Frank was campaigning hard for JFK, he realized he had to back down. He did pay Maltz the full $75,000 for the job. However, he was furious that he had to back down and it was reported that he went on a three-day Jack Daniels binge and totally destroyed his office at the Bowmont House. He also ripped up books and scripts, hurling over bookcases. (Kaplan, 2015) This shows the outrageous reaction of the gamesman when throttled.

## Changes in Style

Sinatra's move from Columbia to Capitol Records between June of 1952 and April of 1953 involved a complex series of creative and personal changes, and culminated in a complete revitalization. After shedding some personal baggage and shifting his base of operation entirely to the West Coast, the singer emerged with a completely new look, attitude, and sound. Gone were the floppy bow ties and slicked hair of yesteryear; in now were stylish cravats of the finest silk and patterns and a jaunty felt hat, a style that communicated sophistication and wit. Not intended to be fancy props, these tasteful touches breathed freshness into his fading image and consequently into his work. A brand new Sinatra had emerged and every inch of this transformation is reflected in his enthusiastic approach to the two main crafts he concentrated on: acting and singing. With an Academy Award for Best Supporting Actor in *From Here to Eternity* under his belt, he was now free to concentrate on revamping his image and re-establishing his position as the world's premier pop vocalist.

Early in 1949, Columbia Records had introduced a new playing medium, the lightweight vinyl "long playing" record (LP). Whereas previous platters were made of a fragile shellac compound (a comparatively rough surface) and spun at a dizzying 78 revolutions per minute (allowing a typical ten-inch pop disc to contain no more than three-and-a-half minutes or so of program material), the new LP was a 12-inch disc with a smoother, quieter plastic surface, traveling at a much slower 33 1/3 rpm. In addition to the incredible improvement in sonic capacity, the new discs also allowed for far greater playing time. Within just a few short years, the 10-inch disc (the standard of the pop music industry from 1949 to 1954) would give way to a 12-inch platter, which offered nearly forty minutes of playing time per side and where the singer could develop the theme album.

Using the two-sided forty-minute album, Sinatra then devised to bring into his recordings particular themes: travel, of course (*Come Fly with Me*, 1958), inner/outer space (*Moonlight Sinatra*, 1966), time and mortality (*September of My Years*, 1965), and most of all, romance and its discontents. In lonely-guy collections such as *In the Wee Small Hours* (1955), *Sings Songs for Only the Lonely* (1958) and *No One Cares* (1959), he makes a depressed kind of yearning seem like the height of urban glamour. It may be no coincidence that Sinatra's take on the torch song occurred at precisely this postwar moment. "It was the decade of the suburban house, the six o'clock cocktail shaker and the regulation grey flannel suit . . . Beautiful love songs served up with lush string backgrounds perfectly reflected the quiet and serenity of the decade." (Levinson, 2001)

More than anybody else, if Sinatra sang a song he made it his: he sounded as if he were making it up as he went along, as if he were writing or even thinking of the words extemporaneously. That's the ultimate in music, to have that kind of intensity, playfulness, and immediacy of emotion, and to be able to convey that to the audience. Sinatra really stands head-and-shoulders above any other singer in this, because he has recorded such a broad range of music, and has been influenced by, and then himself influenced, so many styles. He outlasted just about everybody else, too—the number of years that he recorded and sang is truly amazing. It certainly speaks to his gamesmanship.

While he would work with dozens of talented individuals throughout the sixty-year span of his career, he remained loyal to a relatively small group of arrangers who used his boundless musical energy and insight as a springboard for creating not only his orchestrations (which were usually far superior to any they wrote for other singers), but as the inspiration for their own personal work as well. Sinatra once said that he would never argue with someone like Nelson Riddle on a record date. You respect the arranger because it is also his date.

So many of Sinatra performances advance the idea of eros. There are songs of innocent love deceived, songs of erotic self-deception, self-deception about the lover's own intentions, self-deception about the lover's capacity to weather the storm of romantic loss. There are songs about erotic disappointment and erotic obsession. In some instances, our interest in the subject matter is heightened by a thematic ambiguity created by the special nuances of Sinatra's renderings.

Over the years Sinatra often characterized himself as a saloon singer, meaning in part that he sang in saloons (nightclubs), but also that he sang saloon songs, songs which frequently have bars as their explicit dramatic settings and which present characters in dramatic monologues singing about their romantic disappointments, their pain, their sorrow, their sense of betrayal, their sense of loss, their loneliness, their emptiness, their erotic despair. What makes so much of this music great, in addition to the characteristically superb selection of material and the masterly arrangements, is Sinatra's extraordinary capacity to bring these dramatic situations to life, to convey in song an impressive range of emotions in utterly believable ways: to create a mood of despair, of sorrow, of emptiness, and to render them musically and also conversationally. We really do have the sense, when we're listening to these songs, that someone is there talking to us about his hurt. The saloon song now becomes a plaint, a lament, not just about erotic loss, but about the brokenness of human existence generally, the fallenness of the world, a brokenness of which erotic loss is just one element or expression.

Sinatra sings about despair as well as fulfillment. He sings about love from a perspective assumed after the passage of considerable time. Young love, for example, is viewed from the vantage point of middle age, a theme struck a number of times in the 1965 album *September of My Years* (cute in celebration of Sinatra's fiftieth birthday).). That album includes a song entitled "Man in the Looking Glass," a funny, wistful song about a middle-aged man looking at himself in a mirror and wondering whatever happened to the youthful-looking guy with all the hair. Now what he sees, among other things, is an older man whose sexual desire comically lives in uneasy and unseemly relationship with his age. Yes, old age brings erotic deterioration and decadence and the comedy of the old fool.

He enjoyed nothing but success in the charts, becoming more and more prolific with a remarkable 51 songs cut in 1946 and 72 in 1947. His singing movies kept pulling the customers in, so that by October 1946, in addition to his established routine of winning polls as a record artist (for example, *Down Beat*'s award for favorite singer of 1946), he was voted the most popular film star of the year by *Modern Screen* magazine. Equally indicative was his earning power, where it was estimated that he made $4 million between 1944 and 1946, in addition to the five-year film contract he signed with MGM at a guaranteed $1.5 million plus lucrative residuals, and the $93,000 he was paid for a week of shows in Chicago.

## Sinatra on Film

Sinatra in the 1950's gave us as many credible roles as any actor, from the celebrated street-tough Maggio in *From Here to Eternity* to drug-addicted Frankie Machine in the socially-conscious *The Man with the Golden Arm*. In fact, the edgy, chip-on-the-shoulder characters he loved to play did take on a life beyond the screen and reinforced his public persona of a man risen from the ashes of a bobby-sox career run dry. Sinatra became the aging kid, unbowed, streetwise, but somehow still loyal to his roots and living by his own "Robin Hood" code, a fascinating brigand.

The way he threw himself into his singing career was the way he placed himself mentally into the world of Hollywood. As mentioned previously, he desperately wanted the role of Maggio and he then expressed this deep feeling: "I knew Maggio, I went to high school with him in Hoboken. I was beaten up with him, I might have been Maggio." When Columbia granted him a screen test he flew back from Africa, 27,000 miles, and within 36 hours he was in the studios. He did two scenes—in one of which he played Maggio being found drunk and absent without leave in a hotel garden. Director Fred Zinnemann called producer Buddy Adler to come and see the tests. 'You'd better come down here,' he declared. 'You'll see something unbelievable.' Adler watched Sinatra doing another take, although Zinnemann had no film in the camera. He was just as impressed as the director. Sinatra dreamed, slept and ate his part and he played Maggio so spontaneously that they almost never had to reshoot a scene. Adler felt that Sinatra had the most amazing sense of timing, and occasionally he'd drop in a word or two that made the line actually bounce. Obviously, comparison was made with his singing.

When Sinatra realized that he could have a movie career, he didn't just wing it. In fact, he visited sets, observed directors, and studied the actors.

> "I went around to all the different sets in the studio, and watched the different people work, all the veterans. I'd stand up on a ladder way in the back and picked up pointers from these people. I still have

never had a dramatic coach. I suppose I should have. I almost regret that I didn't."

He went on to describe his attitude toward acting.

"I always try to remember three things as a movie actor. First, you must know *why* you are in the movie, understand all the reactions of the man you are playing, figure out *why* he's doing what he is doing. Secondly, you must know the script...I keep a script in my office, my car, my bedroom, by the telephone, even in the john. And I read the whole script maybe fifty or sixty times before shooting even starts... Thirdly, you must learn and listen to the lines of others; it's no good just learning your own...I have my own technique that I've evolved from discussing acting with some of my chums, like Spencer Tracy and Bogie when he was alive . . . Once we've begun shooting I rarely open the script. If two good actors in a scene listen intently to what the other is saying, they'll answer each other intelligently. Actors who go only by the lines never seem to be listening to the other actor, so the scene comes out on the screen as if you can see the wheels going around in their heads. (Santopietro)

## HIS COMEBACK

"Me," said Frank. "I did it. I'm my own worst enemy. My singing went downhill and I went downhill with it, or vice versa-but nobody hit me in the throat or choked me with my necktie. It happened because I gave no attention to how I was singing. Instead, I wanted to sit back and enjoy my success and sign autographs and bank the heavy cash. Well, let me tell you, nobody who's successful sits back and enjoys it. I found out the hard way. You work at it all the time, even harder than when you were a nobody. Enjoyment is just a by-product of success—you get a kick out of it, fine, but the only real fun in being successful is working hard at the thing that brings you the success. That's what I had to learn. You hear all the time about guys who showed big promise or who even made the top and then suddenly they flub out. Everybody says they must have developed a block or lost their touch or one of the guys at the office was out to get them or whatever. Well, maybe that's just a fancy way of saying the thing I found out: "The only guy that can hurt you is yourself." (Zehme, 1997)

The bobby-soxers were gone and his life had taken a wicked turn; this was the real test, and Sinatra the artist began in earnest. He had to reinvent himself in order to become an enduring classic. The next stages in Frank Sinatra's musical life provide a fascinating lesson on the reversals of fortune. He began the 1950's with no recording contract, no film career, and a passionate but dying personal romance. By the end of the decade he was at the top of two professions — as a musician and a screen actor.

He brought off what must still stand as the most fantastic comeback in show-business history. All of a sudden, the little loser was coming on like a bigger winner than we or he had ever dreamed, the voice sounding great and the man coming on cool, arrogant, exuberant, extravagant, powerful—the Chairman of the Board. This was a man who sensed and understood what an audience craved and wanted.

## Early Style

Frank used the microphone in a way completely unique for the times. Most singers just stood woodenly in front of one and hoped that their voices would be carried to the rafters. Not Sinatra. "They never understood that a microphone is their instrument," Sinatra would say, "It's like they're part of an orchestra, but instead of playing a saxophone, they're playing a microphone."

He would tenderly hold the microphone stand like a considerate lover during romantic ballads, or jerk it roughly if he felt he needed that kind of impact on a brassier number. He would back away from the mike when a dramatic note needed to soar to the heavens and echo, or step into it if he wanted the crowd to hear just the slightest sigh or breath. The girls would swoon in the audience when Frank was onstage, as much for his voice as for the unusual way he performed. The way Sinatra romanced a mike and mike stand was erotic and an important part of his appeal. He was just 5 feet ten and a half, 138 pounds and with a 29-inch waist, but onstage, he somehow seemed like a passionate dynamo, especially when he quivered that lower lip. Paradoxically, he also seemed vulnerable. The total package was irresistible.

He began to take diction classes with instructor John Quinlan in New York in an attempt to lose his New Jersey accent. He wanted to learn to enunciate perfectly when performing, a driven man who would do whatever he felt he had to do in order to make it in the competitive record business and emerge a winner.

Frank spent years trying to determine just how to excel at his craft and capture the public's imagination with all the proper tools, such as breath control, lyrical phrasing, elocution lessons, and even microphone techniques. Sinatra didn't just sing a song; he made it his own. He brought a special agency to his proprietorship. He presented the song like a landscape he'd restored, painting himself into the picture so masterfully that it was impossible to imagine it without him.

The gamesman does not back away from a fight or permit slights to go by without some attack on his opponent. Consider the situation with Lee Mortimer, who had Sinatra arrested and charged with assault and battery and also sued him for $25,000. Louis B. Mayer was disgusted with Frank's behavior and demanded that Frank settle, which he did by giving the reporter $9000. The whole episode put a stain on Sinatra's image and when he appeared at the Capitol Theater he found only a few fans waiting.

## HIS LOW POINT

By now his reputation was going downhill. In 1949, *Downbeat* listed him as the number-five singer. By 1950 he had lost much of his voice. He had to leave in the middle of one performance because his voice gave out. His condition was diagnosed as a submucosal throat hemorrhage.

Yet, in 1951, Frank gave one of his most emotional performances in the studio when he recorded "I'm a Fool to Want You." This session marked a defining moment in the development of Sinatra's interpretative skills. The anguish he felt as a result of his relationship with Ava Gardner is clear with every note in the recording, even though it was never a hit. In June 1952, he was officially dropped by Columbia Records as well as by the talent agency, MCA.

Riddle would later say that Frank was a perfectionist who drove himself and everybody around him *relentlessly*. "You always approached him with a feeling of uneasiness, not only because he was demanding and unpredictable, but because his reactions were so violent." However, Riddle thought of Sinatra as a giant that had the imagination and scope of the rarest kind.

The years at Capitol (1953-61) resurrected Sinatra's career and began his evolution as an artist—he would become a very serious singer who would go on to carefully choose his material. His voice lowered, got better, lost some of its sweetness. His whole attitude was becoming a little more hip. The curly-haired, bow-tied image was gone. Now there was the long tie and the hat.

In 1954 he was named Most Popular Vocalist of the Year by a *Downbeat* poll and his song "Young at Heart" was number one on *Your Hit Parade*. He was named top male vocalist by *Billboard, Downbeat and Metronome*. His comeback was complete when he attended the Academy Awards ceremony on March 25, 1954 and received an Oscar for his role in *From Here to Eternity*. It was astonishing that Frank Sinatra, basically known as a vocalist, would make one of the most dramatic comebacks in entertainment history as an actor. After that he made a number of successful films, including *Suddenly* (in which he played a coldhearted killer, to terrific reviews); *Young at Heart* (as an out-of-work songwriter); *Not as a Stranger* (as a dedicated doctor); and the *The Tender Trap* (as a ladies' man and actors' agent). He also starred in *Guys and Dolls* (as Nathan Detroit), which was a huge box-office success.

In February 1955, he recorded one of his best albums, *In the Wee Small Hours*. The advent of the "long play" allowed Frank to create a mood –whether depressing, with torch songs, or upbeat, with swinging numbers —by recording a series of thematically similar songs.

In time his voice had only gotten better, enriched and emboldened with the songs he would help to make famous over these last few years.

"If the song is a lament at the loss of love," he once said, "I get an ache in my gut, I feel the loss myself, and I cry out the loneliness, the hurt, and the pain that I feel. I know what the cat who wrote the song is trying to say. I've been there and back. I guess the audience feels it along with me."

The Rat Packers loved Sinatra's sense of style, his cool "habits," and his extravagant lifestyle, which is why he was named Pack Master. They marveled about his one hundred suits and fifty pairs of shoes, the fact he carried only one-hundred-dollar bills; anything smaller just didn't matter in Sinatra's world. As Sammy Davis put it, "Whatever he was, he was, above else cool. He was our leader. Nobody did it like Frank. Nobody dared."

Frank's temper and the resulting repercussions only served to enhance his image and added more luster to his celebrity. He was even more admired by his public for his displays of rage, especially if the press constantly derided him about such outbursts. He spoke for his fans. He did what many of them longed to do in their own lives but didn't dare; he didn't take crap from anyone. He fought back for the person who hated his role in life but couldn't do anything about it for fear of losing his or her job; the person treated rudely by a waiter but who could only retaliate by leaving a meager tip; the person whose foot was stepped on in an elevator who could only mumble something angrily incoherent instead of giving the offender a good poke.

In this regard, Irving Goffman, the noted sociologist, made this telling observation, that we come to understand people when they are seen in the context of a performance of a role that is presented to others, *i.e.*, to a team or an audience. The self is composed of two parts: a performer that devises or creates a role and a character whose spirit, strength and fine qualities the performance was designed to portray. We all go through life training for a part and we hope the training pays off and the performance is wonderful. In this sense, Sinatra's performance was so well conceived and executed that he became our dream force, embodying our love, our libido, our hopes and desires. When he sang he created a fantasy of love, loss, pain, devotion, and excitement.

## Artist as a Child Creator

In an interesting work, Freud, in "The Relation of the Poet to Daydreaming," showed that just as children's daydream fantasies are a way for them to fulfill an unsatisfied wish for bodily pleasure, so also in their daydream fantasies, they are able to satisfy precisely those wishes. Now, poets, novelists, dramatists, or even crooners do the same thing as a child at play. They create a world in their imagination. Like the child's play-world, theirs is characterized not by its lack of seriousness, but by its lack of correspondence to external reality. The only difference between the child's daydreaming and the poet's or crooner's is that the former hides his pleasurable fantasies from others, while the latter displays his fantasies for other's pleasure.

The poet John Ciardi once wrote that he didn't deal in ideas but in experiences. He must make illusions for you, and must make something happen, and it must be as if is happening to you. It's as if every experience you try on is another way of seeing yourselves. I must lead you to feel as if you were a child, a lover, a murderer, a dancer, a coward. For only if you try on all your possibilities vicariously can you come to know yourself.

The realm of play is the realm of the image, and therefore the realm of possibility and imagination. Those who cannot play with images are no artists; and those who cannot understand the play of imagery cannot understand art. Play is not only a dimension of living and feeling and willing, but it is, in short, a way of being. Some called it "Dionysian consciousness," which is the view of life as a festival, a dance. The laughter of the child expresses the joy of freedom, of the sense of adventure, of delight, of pleasure. This is what makes Sinatra's music so compelling, if not contagious.

At times, Sinatra was referred to as a playboy. His dalliances with women, drinking, and partying were compulsive, possibly an attempt to deal with some basic conflict. But the metaphor of play fascinates audiences in our time. And in a way, Sinatra was always playing, and even his later films took on this quality. The artist as a player exists most openly to the world when he or she rejects all norms and is bound by boundlessness.

In the summer of 1962, Sinatra embarked on a record-shattering concert tour of Europe called the World Tour for Children, during which he visited children's hospitals and youth centers in Hong Kong, where he donated $95,000 for children's charities: Israel; Greece; Rome; Geneva; Madrid; and London. In ten weeks, Sinatra personally financed thirty concerts and raised more than a million dollars.

At sixty-seven years of age, Sinatra had not slowed down even the slightest bit; the schedule for 1983 was just as demanding. "I don't know how to stop doing things," he said in an interview at that time. "I gotta do something."

One review is particularly revealing. In *The Saturday Review,* Arthur Knight wrote of Sinatra's performance in *The Man with the Golden Arm*.

> The thin, unhandsome one-time crooner has an incredible instinct for the look, the gesture, the shading of the voice that suggests tenderness, uncertainty, weakness, fatigue, despair. Indeed he brings to the character much that has not been written into the script, a shade of sweetness, a sense of edgy indestructibility that actually creates the appeal and intrinsic interest of the role.

He then points out the overlap of Sinatra's artistry in both acting and singing, the coloring of the voice, the mixture of emotions, the ability to improvise and re-create, the combined sense of brashness, vulnerability, elation and despair which surrounds Sinatra.

On 17 April 1973, Sinatra turned up at the White House to sing for the visiting Italian Prime Minister, Giulio Andreotti, and Nixon indulged in rhetoric on the subject of the entertainer. He said: "Once in a while, there is a moment when there is magic in the room, when a singer is able to move us and capture us all, and Frank Sinatra has done that and we thank him ... this house is honored to have a man whose parents were born in Italy, but yet from humble beginnings went to the very top in entertainment."

Whitney Balliett, the music critic, observed, "His phrasing and immaculate sense of timing gave it a poise and stature Crosby's lacked."

Sinatra said of his phrasing, "Instead of singing only two bars or four bars at a time – like most of the other guys around – I was able to sing six bars and in some songs eight bars, without taking a visible or audible breath. That gave the melody a flowing, unbroken quality and that's what made me sound different."

This is from an interview with Bob Dylan, who has just put out a new album of songs from the American songbook.

Question: I noticed that Frank Sinatra recorded every one of these songs. Was he on your mind?

Dylan: When you start doing these songs, Frank's got to be on your mind. Because he is the mountain. That's the mountain you have to climb, even if you only get part of the way there. And it's hard to find a song he did not do. He's the guy you got to check with . . . He had the ability to get inside of the song in a sort of a conversational way. Frank sang to you – not at you . . . Comparing me with Frank Sinatra? You must be joking. To be mentioned in the same breath as him must be some sort of high compliment. As far as touching him goes, nobody touches him. Not me or anyone else.

(AARP Magazine, Feb/Mar 2015, p.24)

In the beginning of the 1960s, Sinatra had a new passion in his life. It was not another "swinging chick"; this was political in nature. During the 1940's he had greatly admired—and named his son after—Franklin D. Roosevelt. Now his on-again, off-again friend from MGM days, Peter Lawford, introduced him to Senator John F. Kennedy from Massachusetts, who was running for President. Sinatra relished being in Kennedy's presence and convinced his friends–the so-called "Rat Pack" (or "The Clan")—to campaign for him. Once again, he was attracted by the supreme aphrodisiac of power. The gamesman in him came alive with this new interest.

Nelson Riddle, in an October 1981 bylined British magazine article, mentioned that Frank had become concerned because his need, at least at one time, was to remain contemporary. He didn't want to be thought of as a star of yesteryear.

In 1957 Nelson returned to writing for a girl singer–a most imposing girl singer—Peggy Lee. The conductor was Frank Sinatra. The idea for the album was Frank's; he brought Lee a list of songs, from which she selected what she wanted to record. She said on a radio show how elated she was to be working with Sinatra and Riddle, saying, "I thought I'd died and gone to heaven. Frank was an excellent conductor, and I'd say, more sensitive to a singer than most. He designed the cover and did the whole production. As a matter of fact, he wanted me to have a misty look on that cover so he had someone spray menthol in my eyes." (Levinson, p. 176).

His whole history shows that Sinatra could at different times be caring and insensitive, classy and tasteless, charming and bad-tempered, tender and tough, family man and player of the field, appealing underdog and unattractive bully.

While on a yacht, Humphrey Bogart's boat *Santana,* David Niven reports that Sinatra began to sing. He sang all night. There were many yachts in Cherry Cove that weekend and by two in the morning, under a full moon, *Santana* was surrounded by an audience sitting in dozens of dinghies and rubber tenders of every shape and size. Frank sang with his monumental talent and exquisite phrasing undimmed by a bottle of Jack Daniels, on top of the piano. He sang till the dew came down heavily and the boys in the listening fleet fetched blankets for their girls' shoulders. He sang till the moon and the stars paled in the pre-dawn sky–only then did he stop and only then did the awed and grateful audience paddle silently away.

Ever since he'd broken out of the no-record period in late 1944 with the smash hit, *Saturday Night Is the Loneliest Night In the Year,* he had enjoyed nothing but success in the charts, becoming more and more prolific with a remarkable 51 songs cut in 1946 and 72 in 1947. His singing movies kept pulling the customers in too, so that by October 1946, in addition to his established routine of winning polls as a record artist (the *Down Beat* award for favorite singer of 1946 was his third consecutive success), he could be voted the most popular film star of the year by *Modern Screen* magazine. His radio series, *Tin Pan Alley,* continued to go great guns at $12,000 per program fee. Equally indicative of his earning power were Kahn's estimate that he made $4 million between 1944 and 1946, the five-year film contract he signed with MGM

## The Ultimate Gamesman

at a guaranteed $11.2 million, plus lucrative residuals and his pay for a week of shows in Chicago.

It was his ability in one mélange to sing as tunefully and resonantly as Bing Crosby, with something of the jazz flair of Ella Fitzgerald and Mel Tormé, and with just as much dramatic power as Tony Bennett, which sets him apart even from these towering artists. Interestingly, he was given more votes than all other nominees put together when 109 jazzmen were asked by *Metronome* in December 1956 to name "The Musicians' Musican of the Year."

At 50 years of age, he put out some of his most brilliant recordings. There was a single, arranged by Gordon Jenkins, *It Was a Very Good Year*, which won two Grammys, one more than the album with a similar theme, *September of my Years*. There was again a touch of the autobiographical in the double album *A Man and his Music*. Sinatra had never made the Top Ten in the 1960's, but *Very Good Year* did, and amazingly three later singles, *Strangers in the Night, That's Life,* and *Somethin' Stupid* (with daughter Nancy) all made Number 1 in America, despite recordings of the Beatles, the Stones, and the Beach Boys, and all in a period when it was almost impossible for good balladeers to make the charts at all.

Sinatra's attempts to cope with rock-pop didn't always work, since sometimes the sentiments were alien to him, and often the language was too, and even the melodic and rhythmic patterns seemed apart from his world. Sinatra's roots were in the 1940's and 1950's, and he always seemed at his best extending that style, the tough little crooner from the tough, hard streets of Hoboken, singing to make it in the world of Berlin, Gershwin, and Cole Porter. He did attempt Rod McKuen or Joni Mitchell songs, but they fell short. But he kept on trying, and while you keep on trying you keep on living.

## GENEROSITY

Sinatra could be very generous in his charitable gestures. For example, in the spring of 1962 he set out on a two-month world tour to raise money for children's charities, having declared himself "an over-privileged adult." He went from Los Angeles back to Los Angeles via Tokyo, Hong Kong, Tel

Aviv, Athens, Rome, Milan, Paris, Monte Carlo, London (where he appeared at the Royal Festival Hall before Princess Margaret), and New York, which is quite a schedule. He paid all expenses, more than $.5 million, and raised more than $1 million. This was still not enough for some of his long-established critics, including *Time* Magazine, which produced a curiously ambivalent piece suggesting that the tour was a stunt to camouflage his unappealing Rat Pack image and to impress President Kennedy. This was certainly a nasty piece of writing, especially after he had raised all this money for a most worthy cause.

Sinatra's generosity and charity, in matters large and small, were quite impressive throughout his life. On May 23, 1976, the University of Nevada at Las Vegas conferred upon him an honorary Doctorate of Humane Letters for his "charitable endeavors which have raised millions of dollars for humanitarian causes and deeds that have frequently been done anonymously."

Sinatra joined a party of 150 celebrities on a visit to Israel in April 1978 for the dedication of the Frank Sinatra International Student Centre at the Mount Scopus campus of the Hebrew University in Jerusalem.

Don Raffell described the November 15, 1956, recording session for the *A Swinging Affair* album: "We had rehearsed the music and we're sitting there. The double doors at Capitol open up and there's Sinatra. He's got a black hat on with a white band, black suit, black shirt, black shoes, white necktie—gangster. He doesn't say anything to anybody, walks into the recording booth and says, "You've had plenty of time to get the balance on this thing. I don't want any fooling around or it'll be your ass!" ... He says that like a hoodlum ... We did one take on each thing that we did. One! That's it. That's all he wanted to do. No slips, no nothing. He was an evil mother!" (Levinson, 2005).

André Previn related the story of the night when he had completed a session at United Recording for which he had written some arrangements. He wandered into the main studio where Sinatra and Riddle were at work, and quietly took a seat in the recording booth:

## The Ultimate Gamesman

"I sat there unseen just in time to hear Sinatra suddenly wheel on Nelson and call him names and belittle him. Nelson was too sweet for his own good. He just took it. He stood there. I couldn't stand it, and I left and went back to my own recording date. About an hour later I met Nelson by the coffee urn, and I said 'Nelson, how can you take that? I mean there isn't anyone as good as you, not anyone in the world, and Frank owes you, as far as I'm concerned, a good fifty percent of whatever success he's had.'

"Nelson said, 'Oh well, you've worked for him, you've written for him. You know Frank—he doesn't even mean it.'" (Levinson, 2005)

Nelson said he was afraid of only one man, and that man was Frank Sinatra, George Roberts related. "Not physically. He was afraid of him because he couldn't figure out what he would do . . . which is why Nelson wanted a first reading every time we played. He wanted it perfect, the first time, so as not to give Frank a chance to not like the chart. If he didn't like them, he'd have to redo them."

Sinatra as the ultimate gamesman was a composite of different temperaments and characters. He was extremely likable and seemed open, yet one always felt in danger of being intimidated by him. He was very seductive and seemingly gregarious, yet when one knew him better, he was introverted and a little lonely. Like the gamesman, he was a collection of seeming paradoxes. He was idealistic, yet shrewd and pragmatic; cooperative, yet highly competitive; enthusiastic, yet he could be detached; earnest, yet evasive; graceful, yet restless; energetic, yet itchy. Serious on the one hand, he was also boyish and playful and could become rowdy.

Some of Sinatra's most dominant values included concern for people, especially those in need, and he would go to extreme lengths to help them out both financially and personally. For him, consideration of others and love were among his most important virtues, while betrayal of a friend was one of the worst evils.

Sinatra had the ability to see details in terms of an overall picture. He could integrate many ideas into his overall plan. We can see that his character, his game orientation, his joy of life, enthusiasm, and dazzling brilliance all served to make him effective as a top performer, recording artist, and movie actor. He was a person of exceptional gifts. He was brilliant, intuitive, and, above all, extremely energetic. One of the early themes in his life was not to give in to authority and to the institutional system. This theme became one of rebellion when he was able to pull this off as a brilliant performer. As an adult, he continued to resent being controlled and dictated to, and more and more he had to be in charge of all the facets of his life. And in the end, even when he couldn't remember the lyrics of the songs that he was performing, he was driven to keep on working and he came to depend upon the excitement of work, of being juiced up by the contest. To the end, he was a gamesman.

CHAPTER FIVE

# His Second Self: The Transformation of Sinatra's Personality Through His Art

No other artist of his genre was so wide-ranging in his scope, so expansive in his vision, so far-reaching in his accomplishments as Frank Sinatra. In more than 60 years of singing, there was hardly a type of American music at which Sinatra didn't excel. He was everything we wanted to be: swinging, moody, sensual, romantic, and even a little dangerous. Sinatra's art and his singing of popular songs, at its best, is rich and fine—and much of the artistry lies in Sinatra's perceptiveness as a singer. Sinatra worked in an interpretive form, singing words set to music by professional songwriters. Because of his sensitivity to the meaning of those words, and his skill at communicating what the lyrics meant to him, he seemed to be engaged not just in interpretation but in spontaneous expression. His records almost sound like an autobiography.

The essential appeal of Sinatra's singing comes from his ability to put everything he had into each song, on every level. He integrated music and emotion as no one else could, to such a degree that it was impossible to extricate one from the other.

Everyone familiar with Sinatra since the 1940's has known that his life off-microphone was a sordid tale of bullying, womanizing, and bad temper, mixed with advocacy for social justice and good deeds done for friends. However, as Gary Giddins (1998) reasons, "Though he may have been, at his much-documented worst, a foul-mouthed misogynist, unthinking lout, violent drunk, friend to criminals, sore loser, and political hypocrite, he was first and last The Voice." (p. 25)

Through his singing. Sinatra was able to evoke an intimate, intense and distinctive experience often not apparent in his everyday life. Sinatra, in his craft as singer-performer, seemed to be not quite the same person as he was in his personal life. On stage, he was able to express and convey a greater range and depth of emotion, mood, vulnerability and tenderness than in his off-stage life. This difference from his performing self and the superficial macho Rat Pack man image suggests that there was a kind of "second self" that he developed, comparable to certain narrative authors, whose self-presentation in everyday life was very different from what they express through their art. Kitty Kelly, in her book, quotes a 1979 *Washington Star* editorial on Sinatra, dizzy with its own mock perplexity: "That such beautiful music should emerge from such vulgarity is one of the great mysteries of the age."

## BACKGROUND

It was Schafer (1983) who introduced the term "second self," to describe the positive aspects of the psychoanalyst's personality in the analytic situation as contrasted with some not-so-admirable qualities appearing outside of the treatment room. The concept was previously described by Fleiss (1942,) who wrote about the analyst's work ego, in which there is a greater facility in using empathy in the analytic setting than out of it. Kris (1952) saw "regression in the service of the ego" as a way of explaining the inspirational aspects of the creative process. However, neither of these discussions fully explains the essential features of the second self. Schafer (1982) thinks Kris missed an essential aspect of the phenomenon, maintaining, "He sometimes seemed implicitly to be endorsing a naively romantic view of the matter—the very opposite of what he was depicting—equating inspiration with simple primitivization." (p. 45).

Schafer (1983) goes on to say that when emotional experience during an artistic performance reflects more admirable qualities than those expressed "off-stage," the "truer" aspects inherent in the second self are being highlighted. According to him, there are many creative writers, who, from what is known about their lives, express more misery, cruelty, greed, snobbery or self-destructiveness than the average person. Yet, these very same men and women may achieve in their writings sublime versions of emotional experience. "Though they are not angels, they write like angels," (p.44), and at their best they make us wish we were like them—or that we had them for friends, parents, or lovers. But in responding to them as creative artists so appreciatively, we are in fact responding to them as *transformed selves*, who have the ability to create an illusion of beings who are basically tender, witty, compassionate, brave, heart-rending, and empathic.

Sinatra, like these creative writers, painters, dancers and performers that Schafer discusses, had this ability in his creative endeavors to bring into being a second "psychic structure"— if you will, a transformed self.

This second self may help to transform ordinary work into creative work, but it may also keep disturbing the harmony of conventional personal patterns owing to the effect of creative disorganization. As a result, the lifestyle of the artist often takes on a quality of restlessness, almost to the point of agitation, that is not evident in the overall life-cycle of the ordinary individual.

Eissler (1971) talks of the way artists approach their work, welcoming the excitation in order to master it through aesthetic form. The artist selects, attends and integrates experience into forms that are most likely to lead to a successful aesthetic solution. The state of excitation arises from a heightened perceptiveness. A painter paints to unburden himself of feelings and visions, as he possesses an inborn greater sensitivity to sensory stimulation.

Freud believed that in the artistic process the ego can unite, modify and fuse split-off psychic elements within itself. This creative integrative process allows for powerful personality transformations to take place. This binding and integration can unify the whole personality, so that the second self can tolerate and permit an array of affects that the first self defends against. In this sense, the second self is freer, in that it can transform aspects of the core personality into a more poignant, general self-presentation. Artistic creation strengthens the self, helps to overcome problems in one's personality, and helps in the mastery of inner and outer reality. Sinatra, then, could be said to ignore or disavow certain attitudes in his first self while he permitted them full rein of expression in his second self. However, despite Sinatra's transitory failures in his everyday life, he did have the ability to shift to another reversible and controllable ego-organization, so that his "second self" is essentially a unified self.

The second self must be distinguished, then, from merely playing a role. A role is a part or character that a salesman or actor assumes in a performance. A role does not have the level of organization, spontaneity, or freedom that we see in the second self. A united and integrated self implies essential qualities, a level of personality identity that is distinct from others. At certain times in analytic work, as when the analyst tries consciously to control countertransference enactments, the work may be more characteristic of a role that is being enacted or the maintaining of a style of behavior, than of the truly expressed second self of the performing artist.

In alluding to the complexity of detailing one's first and second selves, Adam Phillips (1998) writes similarly of Bill Clinton. Should we believe that we are consistent through and through, like actors who are only capable of playing one part? In fact, a person may be able to be the best version of himself as a politician, while in his private life, he may be mendacious. If one's second self is truly at a different level of organization, then it may be the version that succeeds best in a given situation.

When watching Laurence Olivier as Richard III, you know at once that you're not just seeing a façade of an ordinary role-playing actor. You can examine him from any angle and still see the depths of the character he is portraying. You can look deep into his eyes and you won't find Olivier, you see King Richard. Similarly, when you listen to Sinatra singing a song, you are exposed to a comparable variety of emotions and tensions. Sinatra is not acting, but like Olivier, he presents himself at his deepest when he is singing. That is, Sinatra does not really *act* songs so much as he locates their emotional essence, infuses them with his understanding of life, and applies his formidable technique, delivering each song with the spun-out notes of incomparably well-invented phrasing.

Although Sinatra's second self appears in his great artistic renditions to transcend his everyday persona, it is not and cannot be totally disjunctive or discontinuous with his offstage personality. It is a special variant, or transformation of it, assuming a form that integrates selected aspects of his own personality into the constraints required to develop an artistic experience. It is within this form that he is able to express his unique range of feeling. And, as his audiences bore witness to a second persona, they responded in kind.

## Aspects of Sinatra's First Self

The artist has a predisposition, if not an inherent sensitivity, to both intense affect and intense recoil; and this conflicted pattern is pursued throughout life by the struggle to become free of it. In this sense, the artist becomes the prototype of all of us, attempting to express in a greater degree what we all feel. The more effective the struggle against this aspect of expressive emotionality becomes, the more poignant the artistic expression. We all feel some measure of frustrated love, loneliness, and despair. Sinatra is able to express this so intensely and evocatively.

Contrast this sublime characteristic with his everyday character, sometimes bordering on the reckless, hostile and self-assured with an intense vanity and hypersensitivity to insult. In what I term this "first self" presentation, he employs openly aggressive behavior in which even his image as lover may be less in the service of love than of insult to both man and woman. We know that Sinatra was a less than exemplary person if we assume the truth of his biographer's accounts (Kelley, 1986, Taraborreli, 1997). For example, we know from Lauren Bacall's account (Bacall, 1979) that she and Sinatra started going together when Bogart died. The press wrote that Sinatra planned to marry her, a plan which he did imply to her. However, when he saw the item, which he had not given permission to release, he became enraged. He didn't speak to her again for six years and then only in rage. When reporters asked him about the marriage report, he said, "Marriage? What for? Just so I'd have to go home earlier every night? Nuts!" (Kelley, 1986).

His relationships to both men and women seemed characterized by undue ambivalence, and he often experienced them as disappointing and frustrating. Phyllis McGuire (Kelley, 1986) the singer, stated, "Frank had cast other friends aside as cruelly as Jack Entratter. Men like George Evans, Hank Sanicola, Nick Sevano, Joe DiMaggio, Brad Dexter and Peter Lawford, who had loved Frank and stood loyally at his side, suddenly found themselves frozen out of the Sinatra circle for some real or imagined slight" (p. 538-539). Another troublesome trait was his jealousy, which led him to fall in and out of love. This mixture of depression, aggressiveness and envy reveals a specially exaggerated intolerance for loss of love, a fear that led to an extreme diminution in his self-esteem.

He continually had to present himself as a tough guy who hits back at the slightest provocation. For example, he ran into Maxine Cheshire, the society columnist for the *Washington Post* who asked the woman he was dating, his future wife Barbara Marx, about her marital status. Frank politely asked her to leave them alone. Finally, she said, "You are still married to Zeppo, aren't you, Mrs. Marx?" Frank became incensed and called her a "two-dollar broad" and something worse. Then, for good measure, he added that she wasn't worth as much as two dollars and stuffed a single dollar into her glass. There was a great deal of fallout from this incident. In fact, Henry Kissinger called him up the next day to say that he'd overpaid her.

Thus, in his complicated inner life of fantasy and self-representation, he seemed to show evidence of both intense affection and intense recoil that may or may not have been related to the realities of the ways in which he was loved. In another vein, M. Gedo (1980) saw Picasso's disturbed relationships with women as reflecting his relationships in general and perhaps even as a reflection of the way he envisioned reality itself. Like Sinatra, his imaginative experience invested in the artistic creation could engender many problems with those who shared his private life.

## Aspects of Sinatra's Second Self

The second self benefits from those psychic capacities derived from early endowments and talents. We may look at it as an instrument capable of higher integrations of expression and movement. Greenacre (1957, 1958) elaborated on the idea that the intensity of all experiences for the child of potentially great talent means that all the early emotional phases tend to remain more lively and are less decisively settled with age. When these residuals of early phases are revived in later life, they may be disconcerting in their vividness. The gifted person, while knowing the conventional sense of reality, is thus also able to hold it in abeyance in order to explore and concentrate her full powers of integration and imaginative possibilities.

According to this theory, a feeling of loss is at the center of artistic creation (Segal, 1955, Rose, 1987). The creative process has often been seen as a way of mastering and restoring the trauma of loss of the object and artistically recreating the optimal or even idealized connection to it. In the creatively aesthetic rescue from the narcissistic injuries of childhood, the emphasis is shifted from the personal to the universal. What difference would it make if we could trace the development of Sinatra to the artist's frustrated love of his mother?—one could do the same for an accountant in love. What really matters is that the gifted artist has not only the maturity to resolve these conflicts into an artistic portrayal, but also the ability to raise himself to the level of loving his work instead of becoming overly invested in the hatred generated by disappointments in the sphere of love. This mastery is an ongoing process of integration and reintegration.

In these potentialities, we can see a different, second side to the sometimes reprehensible Sinatra, emblematic of sage maturity, where his loving interpretations of lyrics promise and often deliver sensitivity, empathy and perhaps wisdom—the Sinatra of our dreams. Rose (1987, p. 135) sees how "creative work requires the ability to mold and shape, fragmentize, cut off and reunify material—repeatedly; the same form-producing procedures, when carried over to human relations, are dehumanizing." If the artist is not able to confine the creative process to creative work, then he/she will be ruled by it.

We know that among creative people there is often a unique version of the desire to preserve the past, both its painful and pleasurable experiences. In his second self-presentations, Sinatra was able to relive the erotic and aggressive impulses of his childhood by projecting their echoes onto the lyrics he sang to his audience. This process becomes a source of powerful, vicarious gratification for us, and he becomes truly inspired because each song resonates deeply, acquiring universal symbolic meaning, carrying the strong emotional impact of joy and suffering. In his singing he penetrated into the mysterious essence of experience, replete with the powerful memories and emotions that his first self either defensively rejected or could not integrate.

It is the function of the crooner to transmute emotions and to set up in the audience a responsive vibration. Crooning is not only influenced by the audience, it is defined by the audience. The singer who ignores this, through narcissism or lack of talent, is ignored in turn. Sinatra was able to evoke such a resonant and lively sentiment. He was able to locate the emotional essence of his songs, to infuse them with his understanding of life, and to apply his formidable technique, delivering each song in gorgeously spun-out notes.

The creative experience is, after all, to be judged on its sensuousness that awakens feelings and reunites them with thought and perception. The artist attempts to master the past by reshaping aspects of himself in the externalized forms of his work. "What begins as the common task of mastering one's personal past, becomes for the creative artist a process of externalizing and transcending it—to disclose new aspects of reality itself." (Rose, 1987, p. 210). Freud (1911) in "Formulations Regarding the Two Principles of Mental Functioning," writes that the artist is originally someone who turns from reality because of the difficulty of coming to terms with the demand for renunciation of instinctual satisfaction, and who then in the sanctuary of fantasy life allows full play of erotic, ambitious, and other wishes. However, the artist also finds a way of returning from this world of fantasy back to reality, with special gifts that mold fantasy into a new kind of reality.

Further, Freud (1930), in *Civilization and its Discontents*, says that the artist's uncommon predispositions and gifts contain the inherent capacity for transformation of particular underlying emotions into a more or less consciously communicative work. With the release of this energy, there is a heightening of various sexual forces that create an aesthetic pleasure, which is then evoked in the audience.

In all creative work, we are witness to the transformation of the first to the second self. As Schneider (1962) writes,

> Indeed the entire triumph of our lives may be measured by the continuing interpretive transformation of ourselves as long as it is healthy and real—that transformation which expresses itself in so many transcendent ways, not only in works of art and works of science but in all the activities of our social microcosm, and in love and in our children. (p. 93).

The greater the artist, the more emotionally resonant the transformation of primitive content and conflict. The great artists know what to transform, how much to transform, and in what manner to transform, so that playing with art is playing with fire. Such transformations in Sinatra's art are myriad.

Sinatra transforms psychic tension into a form that can excite a sense of movement, of being alive. With his unique gifts, he is able to venture to great heights, to live nearer to his dreams, while simultaneously encompassing the pedestrian and routine. As he ventures beyond the realm of the ordinary, he transports his listeners into the magic of new, ever-changing, ever-subtle, realms of reality.

## IDENTIFICATION

The essential material shaped by artists in their work is derived from an unconscious dynamic in which unsatisfied wishes and longings find expression. Sinatra, like all great artists, is knowingly or unknowingly the interpreter of unconscious themes, and therefore must be finely tuned to the unconscious of both himself and his audience. His relationship to the public is analogous to a transference relationship; and in his empathy for the characters in the songs he sings, he invites the audience to submit their fantasies to him for interpretation. Here you have a relationship between the artist and audience that is much like the situation that takes place in a therapy session.

The struggle between the social or conventional self and the creative self often causes a split in the sense of identity. The balance may swing at times toward the urgency of creative needs, and then shift towards the demands of ordinary life. This could then set up an antagonistic relationship between the conventional and creative identity, as well as within the private world, where the reality sense is held in temporary abeyance until it is reinstated.

In Sinatra's songs, as well as in the areas of his life in which we observe his first self, there is a tension between these two elements. In his crafting of a lyric, he can emphasize creation or surrender, understood in the social context of his time as masculine and feminine. Underlying this dynamic tension is the issue of identification, with special emphasis on the influence of bisexuality. That he can portray so many personal elements of both sexes only highlights how he is able to access them within the realm of his own experience. Interestingly enough, as a very young child, Sinatra was often dressed as a girl, the one that his mother, Dolly wanted. She had bought clothes for a girl and was not going to waste them. Later, at special occasions, she dressed him with pretensions toward elegance: formal dress with top hat and white bow tie. His identity as an adult was indeed captured in the elegance of the clothes he wore and sported.

We might ask how he could express in his singing the prototypical longings and wishes of a woman, if he did not in so doing reproduce aspects of his own unfulfilled and unrepudiated female persona? In his attempt to overcome ambivalent attitudes toward gender, his exquisite identifications with women provide a creative solution. In his work, at its most creative, he projects his inner experience onto a world that he can easily imagine because of his ease in temporarily crossing boundaries of gender identification. This ease, so characteristic of his second self, is rarely to be found in the macho first self that we know in the Sinatra of the Rat Pack.

The poet Carolyn Kizer, who was a teenager at the height of the Sinatra craze in the early 1940's, said that what the girls saw in Sinatra was his vulnerability. He had an androgynous side. If he hadn't been so thin, would the girls have loved him so much? Not on your life. He brought out the mother in them. Sinatra had this sex transience that allowed him to sing a Judy Garland song, and he was always doing that: "The Girl

## His Second Self

Next Door," "I Got It Bad and That Ain't Good." A lot of guys have shied away from singing a girl's song, like "I Could Have Danced All Night" from *My Fair Lady*. Sinatra made it a featured piece of his 1960's concert repertoire.

One could posit that all images and projections born of our fantasy are really nothing but aspects of ourselves. Sinatra, as do other creative artists, goes far beyond the ordinary identification of the maternal and paternal imagoes, as he also includes ones that draw from his ideal self. This aspect acts as a third identification that emerges in the second self. This idealization creates a kind of omnipotent self-love that serves to empower him in his highly personalized rendition of a song. That self-love operates optimally like the "helping-out" ego that Schafer (1983) alludes to when he refers to the analyst who inserts himself, via the psychoanalytic attitude, as a benevolent neutral. It's as if Sinatra had a healing persona within himself.

Most important, this third identification, acting like a third eye and ear, can come through in the second self not only as consciously unseen and unfelt, but as a critical and inevitable act in the process of creativity. So, beyond the bisexual identifications, Sinatra is able to invent, if not pioneer, many other identifications unique in his rendering of powerfully emotional relationships. Freud was careful not to explain artistic creation as an outcome of neurosis. In the way that Sinatra is able to transform himself in song, his achievement as a singer matches the painter's feelings for texture, the dramatist's command of tension, the architect's dedication to structure, and the poet's sensitivity to words. As I see it, among creative artists, there is an intuitive working together of preconscious and conscious ego functions to produce the final personal mode of artistic expression.

Sinatra, a model of the true artist, uses this third creative identification with relative ease, whether consciously or unconsciously, to facilitate his enactment of any role, male or female. As he identifies himself with both genders, he projects that identification into his singing. The passion and the exactness for the proper line, balance, rhythm or phrasing all draw from this third identification, which is then invested in the artistic experience. By means of this process, he was able to capture reality in all its subtle interrelationships; otherwise, the songs would have become like the stereotyped and repetitious renditions of lesser performers.

Sinatra becomes so much stronger in his second self when he is able to abandon self-love for the fortunes of his artistic journey. His artistic expression is the sublimation of this eternal, inner longing. His quest for exactness of expression, for changing the form of a passage or highlighting certain phrasing, arises from this never fully-satisfied urge. The struggle for his own musically unique presentation of the world is the struggle for identification in sublimated form. And it was this sublimation, arising from multiple and complex identifications, that became the signature of his second self and produced a degree of tenderness, sympathy, and hurt in this oddly gentle baritone that women loved and with which they identified. Listening to "Try a Little Tenderness," we hear a wise young man advising the world's husbands to be kinder and gentler.

Orson Welles, in a tribute to Sinatra, cited the singer as giving us a present of his vulnerabilities (Shaw, 1982). I would add that Sinatra's gift of his vulnerabilities often relates to difficult-to-bear emotions, such as the pain of his own unfulfilled love and of efforts at loving. Vulnerability also underlies his being out there and taking risks. Within his otherwise rather macho first persona, Sinatra cannot reveal his more tender second self. This ability in vulnerability to appeal, engage, and seduce has been the hallmark of certain specially-gifted performing artists over time.

## THE TRANSFORMATION OF HIS PERSONALITY THROUGH HIS ART

As an artist, Sinatra projected one overriding theme: loneliness. Hamill (1998) writes that all of his ballads are strategies for dealing with loneliness. When we look into his songs, we find themes that constantly deal with women who got away, abandonment, the loss of love, or with misunderstandings that never can be rectified. Sinatra was an only child growing up in a neighborhood of large families. Hamill quotes him, "I used to wish I had an older brother that could help me when I needed him. I wished I had a younger sister I could protect. But I didn't. It was

## His Second Self

Dolly, Marty and me" (p.70). We have only to think of how he transforms and infuses the sentiment in "Soliloquy" from *Carousel*. Here he sings of the father who guides and provides strength for the boy and also supports and nourishes the girl.

Further, he told Hamill, "There's nothing worse when you are a kid than lying there in the dark. You got a million things in your head and nobody to tell them to." As an artist, his audience makes up for that deprivation and he continues time and time again to tell his story to this audience.

Sinatra was influenced by Crosby, but there are clear differences between the two. Crosby was self-contained, and when he sang it was as if he were singing to himself. Watch him singing "True Love" to Grace Kelly in *High Society*—he's barely acknowledging her presence as he sings to the horizon. It's a performance in marked contrast to Sinatra's erotic murmur of "You're Sensational," sung directly to Kelly in the same film. Sinatra wanted and needed to make a direct personal connection with the audience. The loneliness pouring out of Frank informed his art all along the way, both in the recording studio and on film.

In telling the audience his story, he has a great ability to connect by making each person feel as if he were singing to him or her alone. When he voices this intimacy in his singing, he actually does make each song sound like a very personalized part of his life. Where other singers, at best, work with lyrics and melodies, Sinatra deals, in addition, with mental images and pure feelings.

"Frank's appeal is so great and so wide, I think because it boils down to one thing: You believe that he's singing (directly) to you," explained Frank Military, Sinatra's former right-hand man. He continues:

> If you go to any of the concerts, you'll find truck drivers and prize-fighters and all kinds of people, and they just go crazy over him. You'll see people that were there from the beginning, his original audience, all those older folks who were there at the Paramount in 1941, and 1942. You can talk to them, as well as to the new audience that he gets, the young kids today, and every one of them swears that Sinatra sang to them personally. (Friedwald, 1995)

Sinatra, in the beginning, was tame; he didn't gesture, swing his hips, stamp his feet, or leap in the air. He just stood at the microphone, clutching it as if he were too frail to remain standing without it. But the mike mannerisms, the limp curl, the caved-in cheeks, the lean, hungry look, and the frightened smile all emphasized a boyishness that brought him as close as the boy next door.

Sinatra often said that he was strongly influenced by Billie Holiday. He felt that Holiday had the capacity to make each song hers, and he often said, "She lived inside the song. It didn't matter who wrote the words or the music. She made it hers. She made them her story."

Sinatra does the same. He inhabits a song the way an actor inhabits a role, bringing his own life to the music. That is why he can craft the songs he sings into a short story. It is as if he is telling his own personal story through the lyrics. Thus, many of the songs he sings became his signature songs. They are Sinatra's songs.

The story in a song is his first priority. He stresses certain words upwards or downwards and holds the notes of others to heighten the drama. For example, songs like "Where or When" culminate in an intensity, a climax, that magnifies the drama; he holds us to it and moves us along to this climax with a dramatic effect.

He consistently altered melodic lines to a jazz style that became uniquely his own. His swinging improvisations individualized nearly any piece of music he interprets. His musical sensitivity permitted him to swing the melodies in such a manner that they became a potent musical instrument.

Sinatra was at once a great actor and a great musician. With each song he effectively created a new character. He shifted from attitude to attitude with every new text in the way that singers normally use different keys for each tune. In this mode of musical transformation and progression he engendered a special kind of warmth, tenderness and sensitivity. In some of the early tunes, such as "Someone to Watch Over Me" and "I Don't Know Why" he presented himself more as a forlorn, lost soul than as the kind of predatory wolf he would play in later years. In an early song from the movie *Anchors Away* he sang "I Begged Her," much like a sheep in wolf's clothing.

## His Second Self

With all that he finally achieved for himself, in his music he expressed a consuming emptiness, an almost grieving personal unhappiness. There was a risk in this attempt because he had to deliver an authenticity of emotion rather than the empty technique of the virtuoso. More than a wish to be admired, his singing demanded to be felt, revealing more than it concealed.

## His Singing Technique

The incredible phrasing in the vocal techniques Sinatra employed to express powerful emotions may be overlooked or taken for granted, until you sing along with a recording and find yourself gasping for air as he casually plots a sixteen-bar phrase with one exhalation.

His street-tough persona was irresistibly softened by an artistic control in which his voice was transformed, its extraordinary clarity and directness sharpened for expressive purpose, so that even the residual Hoboken inflections achieve eloquence. When he stepped into a song, the manners of a punk were instantly abandoned for those of an overpowering troubadour, causing us to wonder if the offstage Frank were a bit embarrassed by his profession. He made singing a manly art, but a complicated one—sexual, aggressive, physical, vulnerable, sadistic, masochistic, disturbing. How are we to reconcile the man who sings "Night and Day" on *Sinatra and Strings*, to choose one of many examples, with the concert performer who demeaned women reporters as "whores of the press"?

Sinatra certainly learned a great deal from his years with Tommy Dorsey, especially about breath control and phrasing. Listen to his 1941 recording of "Without a Song." At the end of the bridge, Sinatra goes up to a mezzo-forte high note to create the phrase– 'as long as a song is strung in my SOUL!' But he does not breathe then, as most singers would. He drops easily to a soft 'I'll never know . . .' This linking of phrases between the inner units, learned from Dorsey, gave Sinatra's work a kind of seamlessness." (Hamill, 1998).

Compare him in this respect to the other popular singers of the time. Before Sinatra, songs were just sung straight and without much panache.

What is impressive is the beauty and subtlety of the voices, although there is little differentiation between songs. Listen to Perry Como. He has a magnetism in his voice, but what seems to vary is usually only the tempo. Or to Johnny Ray, who tears into each song with intense passion. Yet, these passions hardly ever varied or shifted, so his performances just repeated earlier editions of themselves.

Sinatra had many tricks, like the funny little sliding, skimming slur he did coming off the end of a note, as in "All . . . or nothing at all . . ." Early on, he created a sensation with his rendition of "The Music Stopped." He changed the phrasing, which charged the song with such heightened sexual tension that it left the audience in a frenzy. Listening to "Let Me Love You Tonight" or "Guess I'll Hang My Tears Out To Dry," we can see how he played with the lyrics as if he owned them.

It was with Nelson Riddle that Sinatra struck his most consistent balance between toughness and *angst*. *Songs for Young Lovers (1954), Close to You (1956)* and especially *In the Wee Small Hours* may contain Sinatra's warmest ballad performances, sustaining a mood of quiet intimacy and reminiscence. His rendition of "I've Got you Under My Skin," which Sinatra and Riddle jauntily syncopated against a light, finger- snapping beat, becomes not the sophisticated yet abject confession of love that Cole Porter's lyrics imply, but the fond tribute of one sensualist to another. In the song's climax, Sinatra admits that for the moment he's a smitten fool, and this exhilarating expression of a perfect balance between intoxication and wry knowingness may be the apex of all his swinging music.

Of course there were other singers who had an undeniable appeal to women—Al Jolson, Rudy Vallee the Vagabond Lover, and Bing Crosby, whose enormous record sales built the fledgling Decca Record Company—but none ever swept audiences off their feet as Sinatra did, producing in them a hysteria of ecstasy. He brought sex into the lyrics. No one before him made so blatant a use of songs as an instrument for accompanying lovemaking. Sinatra never just sang; he seduced. The hysteria that created resulted from his uncanny ability to project an enormous sexual excitement, leaving young bobby-soxers moaning, sobbing, panting or screaming ecstatically.

His songs portrayed a tender lover as well as a vulnerable one. When he suffered because *No One Cares*, as he titled one of his albums, or, when he was "a fool to want her" in the wee hours of the morning, his anguish was so palpable that his listeners wept with him and for him. The song embodied his tormented relationship with Ava Gardner, the great love of his life. The 1951 recording of "I'm a Fool to Want You" was done in one take. He left the studio spent.

It was not just on the levels of ecstasy and heartache that he grabbed his listeners. The pitch of his singing was equally intense when he was upbeat and buoyant and sang "Come Fly with Me" or "New York, New York." Singing was then an unabashed expression of sheer joy.

## HIS LIFE AS A DRAMATIC PRESENCE

Sinatra reinvented himself and took on the portrayal of a fighter who is knocked down but gets up and goes on to win. He alienated the Hollywood press, calling them "whores and pimps" (Taraborrelli, 1997). In 1946, the Hollywood Women's Press Club gave Sinatra the *Least Cooperative Actor* award. He punched out the columnist Lee Mortimer, who constantly criticized him. Because Sinatra was a devoted Roosevelt supporter, the Hearst newspaper chain talked about his Communist leanings. They also reported that he enjoyed friendships over the years with the Mafia.

As mentioned before, what came next were the losses of his movie contract, his radio show, his recording contract, and his agents. And then in the spring of 1950, near the end of a eight-week engagement at the Copacabana nightclub in New York, as mentioned before, he lost his voice. He got it back later that year but by then he was on the decline. His negative attitude toward women and his abandonment of his wife and the flaunting in public of Ava Gardner were seen as being too cruel to women. This core audience of women who left him became a source of pervasive, contaminating anguish. More than many other performer, he needed the audience; he needed them to ratify his existence and needed to feed on their emotions.

The bobby-soxers were gone and his life had taken a wicked turn; the real test of Sinatra the artist began in earnest. He had to reinvent himself to become an enduring classic. The next stages in his musical life provide a fascinating lesson in the reversals of fortune. He began the 1950's with no recording contract, no film career, and a passionate but dying personal romance. By the end of the decade he was at the top of two professions—as a musician and a screen actor.

Although Gardner and Sinatra never worked together, she interceded on his behalf with Columbia's president, Harry Cohn, to help her husband land the part in *From Here to Eternity*. And Gardner in her alcoholic, reclusive later years was supported by Sinatra. In 1949, MGM let Sinatra go. In 1950 George Evans died, at the age of forty-eight. In 1952, *Meet Danny Wilson* flopped and Universal refused to renew Sinatra's option for a second film; he was dropped by Columbia Records; CBS cancelled *The Frank Sinatra Show*; and he was released by his theatrical agency. "I did lie down for a while and had some large bar bills for about a year." Then he said to himself, "O.K, holiday's over, Charlie. Let's go back to work."

The great fighters always got up after they were knocked down. And Sinatra, embodying a first-rate fighter, got up. With his role in *From Here to Eternity*, he won an Oscar for Best Supporting Actor, and he came back. Think for a moment of his rendition of "That's Life," in which he sings, "I pick myself up and get back in the race." F. Scott Fitzgerald said, "There are no second acts in American lives," but Sinatra proved him wrong; he had the greatest second act in show-business history.

More and more, men identified with the personal drama of the fall. Sinatra had paid his dues. He then made his historic album, *In the Wee Small Hours*. The essence of the lyrics was that in spite of loss, abandonment, and defeat, what was important was getting through the night. And what you faced was another day, a new woman, and another chance to roll the dice. There was much regret but there was no self-pity. In the end, his most durable expression, his salvation, lay in his music. That was his message.

The singer's emphatically aggressive vocals are a sharp reminder that fifty years ago Sinatra was the first white American pop singer to inject quirky personal feelings and a sense of erotic intimacy into a polished but bland pop-crooning tradition. In the mid-1950's, a more mature Sinatra reinvented himself, and in the process defined the image of the grown-up pop singer as a hip urban sophisticate with a streak of romanticism under a swinger's façade.

With the passage of time there were even more ways that his second self developed, enabling him to integrate a greater range of emotional intensity into his performance. With James, Dorsey, Stordahl, and even Riddle, Sinatra sang in a pure, tender and vulnerable style. In later years, he allowed more aggression and force into his songs. When he performed at Madison Square Garden in a 1974 concert, *The Main Event*, Howard Cosell, the boxing broadcaster, was picked to introduce him. In fact, the stage was set as a fight ring and the cover of the album had Sinatra with both hands raised like a victorious fighter. He started singing, "I've Got You Under My Skin," with the full power and force of a singer transformed from his early days. Screams erupted from the audience with many women in the front rows yelling. Sinatra smiled, looked down, and said, "Where does it hurt you, baby?" It was clear that the triumph of his second self had fully evolved.

In fact, he recorded many renditions of songs at different points in his life, for example, "I'll Be Seeing You." At the time of later recordings there is a tougher, more masculine approach. He becomes the consummate artist, consolidating in a cohesive self a vast array of affects and attitudes.

Discussing one of his Carnegie Hall concerts, Stephen Holden said,

> "The most remarkable thing about Mr. Sinatra in the autumn of his years is the emotional volatility he continues to project onto whatever songs he touches. Unlike the vast majority of seasoned pop singers, Mr. Sinatra doesn't try to hold onto an image of his younger self. He may have performed the same springs directly out of the moment and situation at hand." (Mustazza,1998 p. 187).

Further, Holden writes that the one thing that made Sinatra, at seventy-four years old, a riveting performer was the spontaneity of phrasing and intonation he brought to almost everything he sang, no matter how many hundreds of times he sang them.

Sinatra's appearance on stage was usually awaited with hushed anticipation, and his entry provoked gasps and gurgles of excitement. The spell he wove was a disparate combination of gentleness and roughness, of vulnerability and violence, of compassion and coarseness, whose dialectical interplay added a dazzling dimension to his work. Heightened by artful showmanship, these elements attracted audiences that were not part of the swooning syndrome, and were not privy to his thunderous emergence into the world of popular music.

Sinatra had a penchant for making his singing a form of autobiography that touched new groups as he entered new phases of life. *September of My Years*, the album that marked his fiftieth birthday, dealt with the loss of innocence, of youth, and young love. He was a man in his prime looking backward and wondering, "Where is the star that shone so bright? . . . Why must the moments go by with such haste? . . . The world I knew is lost to me . . . Where did it go? . . . And now the days grow short . ," .Was that a reason why he wooed and married a woman (Mia Farrow) who was younger than two of his children?

When he recorded "That's Life," a world-weary look at living, there was resignation in its existentialist voice. Several years later, just before his father died, he cut "My Way." It made its impact not only because of the assertion of his self-willed, indomitable course in life, but also because the song was framed by the line, "And now the end is near."

Along with this poignant self-expression grew the kind of relationship that only Sinatra was able to construct with his audience, the audience that stuck by him for sixty years. That audience grew up with him and he in turn became intertwined with their lives. They drank listening to him, danced to his voice, fantasized while he was singing, and made love while his voice filled the room. He invented an illusion and created a highly imagined, almost dreamlike storyline.

For sheer dramatic effect and a show of artistry never before witnessed in a singer's performance, think of the concert of June 13, 1971, his announced retirement concert. According to Shaw, author of *Sinatra, The Entertainer*, first, Rosalind Russell came onstage and after some entertainment, signaled the approach of the evening's climactic moment. Struggling to keep her voice under control, Miss Russell, in shining rhinestones on white crepe, announced, "This assignment is not a happy one for me." Her voice cracked, "Our friend has made a decision"—she fumbled for words—"a decision we don't particularly like but one which we must honor. He's worked long and hard for us for thirty years with his head and his voice," she sighed, "and especially his heart. But it's time to put back the Kleenex and stifle the sob, for we still have the man, we still have the blue eyes," she paused, "those wonderful blue eyes, that smile. And for the last time, we have the man, the greatest entertainer of the 20th century..."

When Sinatra came onstage, waving a finger and cautioning her softly, "Don't you cry," the audience leaped to its feet—the first of three standing ovations and the start of an emotion-racked interplay between performer and audience.

During the singing of "Nancy (With the Laughing Face)," his eyes filled with tears. The words of "My Way"—"I face the final curtain"—brought a ripple of sighs from the audience. Barbra Streisand, by then in a seat in the orchestra, dabbed her eyes with a handkerchief. As the song ended, Sinatra was given a second standing ovation. Having delivered the existential, "That's Life," Frank now chose for his final number "Angel Eyes," because, as he explained, "It's a saloon song and I've been a saloon singer." As he began the song, the stage was darkened, and he was picked up in a dramatic silhouette by a pin spot. He staged the finale with style and feeling. Mid-song, he lit a cigarette. He exhaled and the smoke billowed around him. He was building toward the last of the song. "'Scuse me while I disappear," he sang. The spin spot of light blinked out—and he was gone.

> The suddenness of the departure stunned the teary-eyed audience. There was a shocked moment of silence, and then thunderous applause crashed through the theater as the audience once again leaped to its feet. This exit was cited as "the single most stunning moment ever witnessed on a stage." Sinatra returned for one, two, three curtain calls. The audience wanted more songs. But he would not do an encore. Sammy Davis, Jr. bounded on the stage, dashed into the wings, and led Sinatra out, feigning anger. The applause

rose to a new crescendo. He embraced Frank, who turned to the audience, and said "Love you all," blew a kiss of thanks—with many ladies instinctively reaching for their compacts—and was gone. (Shaw, p. 44).

## THE SECOND SELF: SOME FINAL THOUGHTS

I chose the second self as an organizing construct in an effort to grasp the sometimes enigmatic marvels of Sinatra's impact. The dramatic effect of his performance, the expressive, moving, touching and emotive potent force of his singing, make us wonder how we are to understand and explain our idealization of Sinatra the man and his art. Other singers move their audiences, but it is Sinatra who involves us in the story of his life, his loves and failures, his growing old, the loss of youth, his vulnerabilities and tenderness, his yearning and sadness—all of which flow forth from a person who does not display this magnificent repertoire of emotions when he is away from the microphone. These emotions must, of course, must be latently there, but are not as accessible and most certainly not well integrated in the first self, in which they are split off in a defensive pattern.

Yet, once he stepped onto the stage or was in a recording studio, and began a song, he showed an uncanny ability to penetrate, fuse, and connect with split-off emotions and concerns with which everyone could identify. It is not that the equally personal, but different, first self cannot create its own set of illusions with its public appeal, as we see in the Sinatra of the Rat Pack. However, it was only via the transformed second self that he was able to reach such heights and depths of musicality and humanity. It is not even that the second self is in some absolute sense a "better" self, although by now it should be clear that I personally prefer it, since it is a more creative and fuller one. However, it is better for performing purposes: there is a uniquely personalized contact with his audience as the creative process enables him to explore feelings that most genuinely are there, but paradoxically, in a make-believe, but altogether "real," world of the artist's creation.

Music is a creative transformation of feeling into form. In this artistic creation a greater range of emotion becomes more available, better tolerated, more complex, and more effectively expressed. There is an inner integration of feelings with thought and perception. Art reunites perception and affect by strengthening the integrative function of the self and overcomes conflicts in the self.

Assessing his own abilities in 1963, he sounded a note that was quintessentially Sinatra: both forlorn and tough. "Being an 18-karat manic-depressive, and having lived a life of violent emotional contradictions, I have an over-acute capacity for sadness as well as elation," he said. "Whatever else has been said about me personally is unimportant. When I sing, I believe, I'm honest."

CHAPTER SIX

# The Man of Action and Conflict

There are a number of avenues that we can take in approaching the complex life of Sinatra. Many writers have already focused on some of the more undesirable aspects of his life, or what we can refer to as underlying negative character traits. Everyone familiar with Sinatra since the 1940's has known that his life off-microphone was a sordid tale of bullying, womanizing, and bad temper, mixed up with the promotion of social justice and good deeds done for friends. How can we reconcile the exquisite delicacy of say, Sinatra's performance of "Try a Little Tenderness," with numerous examples of his punching out those who he thought were insensitive or crude?

A school of Sinatra devotees, among them the well-intentioned Jonathan Schwartz, have argued that the tawdry details of Sinatra's private life are irrelevant to his music, that the Voice was all that is important. This is essentially the tack that Will Friedwald follows in assessing Sinatra's genius. However, other schools of Sinatra detractors, including the biographers Anthony Summers and Robbyn Swan, define Sinatra largely by his rough and aggressive behavior. For them, the voice goes unheard. Possibly, the potency of both points of view—and, more significantly, the tension of their fundamental irreconcilability—seems to be the secret of Sinatra's uniqueness and enduring appeal. It is virtually impossible for the mind to hold, simultaneously, the conflicting realities of Sinatra's crudeness and his sensitivity, though we know them both to be real. The facts of Sinatra's biographies do not nullify his art, but contradict it; and there's something compelling, even poetic, in that contradiction.

When we look at a person's life and try to focus on exactly what defines that life or what constitutes its important elements, we have to make particular decisions about what we are going to highlight. Do we primarily emphasize the character or qualities that the person exhibits in various phases of their life, the stuff that made them likeable or undesirable, or do we follow the paths they took toward their success and their actions throughout their life, what they strived for, and what they attained?

These two parts of a person's life have been labeled by Aristotle as *ethos* (character) and *mythos* (the combination of the incidents or actions in a person's life). In all, according to Aristotle, *mythos* is the most important element. Much has been written about Sinatra's personal life, the unpleasant elements of his character, as well as his heightened sensitivity. And, often, his gifted and unique talents have been given second place. But we ought to look at what Aristotle says about this: "Tragedy is essentially an imitation not of persons but of action and life, of happiness and misery. All human happiness or misery takes the form of action; the end for which we live is a certain kind of activity, not a quality. Character gives us qualities, but it is in our actions—what we do—that we are happy or the reverse." (Aristotle, *Poetics*, p. 675).

So in essence, Aristotle is saying that the life and soul of a person's story are in the actions they take in moving their life forward, and the issues surrounding their character; the likeable or unlikeable qualities come second. In fact their actions become the design and intention of their lives. It is the events in a person's life that make for its plot. So for Sinatra, the story of his life should not be defined by theme or character, but rather by his actions, accomplishments and the deeds that he performed. His character has a different significance and in some ways underlies his activity, yet the actions he performed give his life the dimensions that capture his audience.

Desire is always there at the start of one's story, often in the state of initial arousal—he wanted to be a singer—often reaching a state of such intensity that movement must be created, action undertaken, and change begun. The defining characteristics of Sinatra's life, his aspiration, desire to get ahead, strivings, and ambition provide us with the theme of his life and become the dominant dynamic of his story, a force that drives him forward.

## AMBITION

Ambition may be the defining characteristic of successful people. Ambition is the force that drives the person forward and acts as a vision of what he wants to accomplish. It creates conditions in which he strives to have more, to do and to be more. Sinatra must be seen as one of the most ambitious figures in modern entertainment. It seems that whatever he touched or imagined he attained. In fact, his ambition was the dominant theme in his life, a force that drove him upward. He acted as if he were a "desiring machine," as his needs and wants constantly became larger and larger.

It is difficult to talk about ambition without considering the underlying aspect of motivation. While ambition instills in us a generalized hunger to succeed in life, there are different paths and ways to succeed, and we can call all of these the paths to success. And so it is the strength of these needs within us that creates what we speak of as motivation.

## MOTIVATION

As motivation has been studied over and over again, it has become clearer what is meant by the term. McClelland has been the leader in this analysis; and he has shown that there are three aspects or needs in the theory of motivation: 1) achievement; 2) power; and 3) affiliation (relationships).

Here are some of the issues underlying these needs.

> **NEED FOR ACHIEVEMENT:** I set difficult goals for myself, which I attempt to reach; I work intensely at everything I undertake.
> **NEED FOR POWER:** I feel that I can dominate a social situation; I always strive to be in control, and I usually influence others more than they influence me.

**NEED FOR AFFILIATION:** I am in my element when I am with a group of people who enjoy life; I go out of my way just to be with my friends.

When we consider these three needs as a template to examine Sinatra's life, we can understand how he became such a dominating figure. He excelled in all three of these qualities of motivation. We know that he was extremely concerned both with recording the best songs and enlisting the best personnel to help him in this. When it came to acting, he excelled in a number of important roles that showed his talents. He was driven to be the best he could be. Next is the need for power, in which the individual wants to be in control of his life, as well as exerting influence over others and having an impact himself. Here again, Sinatra is out in front. He controlled his own music label, had a dominating interest in Las Vegas, and was possessed a number of businesses. After a while, he was in total control of both the songs he recorded and the movies he played in, much more than any other entertainer. Lastly, when it came to relationships, he was surrounded by an entourage of important people who followed him and swore him their allegiance. He also made sure that he befriended Presidents as well as the major and important figures in the world. So, in this sense, Sinatra hit the bullseye in all three aspects of motivation.

The interrelationship between power and achievement is important to understand, because someone high in power motivation and low in achievement could get himself elected to an important position and then do very little after that. There have been presidents who accomplished very little in office, while others were constantly involved in major projects that produced important results. More than any other vocalist, Sinatra set forth to establish his impact, control and influence over his world at large.

## THE ACHIEVEMENT MOTIVE

Motivational systems generally govern our behavior. The achievement motive represents a recurrent concern about doing something better.

People high in this motive are attracted primarily to situations where they can see how to improve themselves. They want to have personal responsibility for their outcomes and need feedback that tells them how well they are doing.

Entrepreneurs are people who are high in this motive. In fact, since efficient business activity is a key element in the economic success of individuals and nations, it is not stretching the evidence too far to suggest that the achievement motive has a lot to do with wealth and poverty or the standards of living people enjoy. In following Sinatra's life, it is quite evident how concerned he was about his own improvement, which is why he insisted on enlisting the best talent there was in the music business. He also realized the importance of hiring composers and lyricists who would produce their material only for him. He was an entrepreneur *par excellence* and this is often overlooked in analyzing his life. He was more achievement-oriented than most of the other singers and that is the reason his recordings have held up over the years. He was constantly focused on improvement, which is a large part of his distinction and prominence.

Whether working with Nelson Riddle, Billy May, or Gordon Jenkins, Sinatra always surrounded himself with the best in the studio, in his arrangers, producers, musicians, engineers. Not only was he talented in his own right, but he learned early on in his career something many artists of his stature never figure out, that other people have imagination and vision, too. What's really fascinating is that despite the input of various composers, lyricists, arrangers, band members, and all of the other recording personnel, Sinatra's records still come across as intensely personal statements. Moreover, his private complexities and the often-poor choices he made in his personal life notwithstanding, Frank always made sound choices when it came to his art.

On January 6, 1961, John F. Kennedy sent his private plane, the *Caroline*, for Frank Sinatra and Peter Lawford so that they could spend the next two weeks planning the pre-inaugural gala in Washington. According to his daughter Nancy, in what has to be one of the most astonishing cases of Frank doing it "his way," "Dad wasn't fazed by the news that Laurence Olivier and Ethel Merman couldn't make the date of the inaugural because they were appearing on Broadway in *Becket* and *Gypsy*, respectively. He bought all of the seats and closed the shows for that night in both theaters."

For the inaugural, Sinatra assembled a stellar cast for the gala, some of whom flew long distances to take part. Participants included Olivier and Merman, Leonard Bernstein, Sidney Poitier, Anthony Quinn, Joey Bishop, Louis Prima, Keely Smith, Juliet Prowse, Helen Traubel, Ella Fitzgerald, Gene Kelly, Nat King Cole, Milton Berle, and, of course, Sinatra himself.

Afterward, he spent time at the Kennedys' compound in Hyannisport with Pat Lawford and Ted Kennedy. On one of those days, Frank, the President, and other friends and family members went cruising for three-and-a-half hours off Cape Cod on the *Honey Fitz*. He was totally in his element; he had risen to the top.

In 1981, there were further rumors about alleged Mafia connections. President Reagan had been moved to write a letter in defense of his friend. "I have known Frank Sinatra for a number of years," said Reagan. "I am aware of the incidents, highly publicized quarrels with photographers, nightclub scrapes, etc. and I admit it is not a lifestyle I emulate or approve. However, there is a less-publicized side to Mr. Sinatra which justice must recognize. I know of no one who has done more in the field of charity than Frank Sinatra." A letter of recommendation from the President of the United States certainly places a person at the top of the ladder.

## THE POWER MOTIVE

A high need for power is associated with an interest in attaining and preserving prestige and reputation. This motive leads to more openly competitive and assertive behavior. From reviewing the research on this motive, we get the impression that the power motive is something of a Hydra-headed monster that shows very different faces depending on the situation.

One glitch arises when high power needs are associated with a high or low degree of inhibition. Men who are high in power and low in inhibition think in terms of personally dominating others. They tend to drink too much and play the role of Don Juan, trying to seduce as many women as possible. When Sinatra's power needs were mixed with low inhibition, he would act out by striking out, and in so doing would take on some of the characteristics of the image of Satan. However, when his power needs were under control, he would appear to possess some of the characteristics of the image we have of God. He would act by exercising his power on behalf of others and do good by them. He was certainly less impulsive and more self-indulgent. He would take over leadership positions, as he did for the presidential inaugurations. He became a very responsible citizen, but this could change very quickly, which is what made him such a conflicted individual. However, this behavioral change would also add to his charisma—no one could figure how he was going to respond.

## High Relationship Needs

The Sinatra household came to life when he entertained other guests, which was at least once a month and sometimes more. For dinner parties, the Sinatras would often hire as many as twenty-five workers to cook food and otherwise prepare the home for dinner parties. The guest list—usually there would be around forty people—would read like a "Who's Who" of show business, the Gregory Pecks, the Chuck Connors, Merv Griffin, Robert Wagner and Jill St. John, Steve and Eydie, Roger Moore, Barbara's son, Bobby, and of course Nancy, Frank Junior, and Tina.

At the parties, Frank and Frank Junior would sit at the bar for hours drinking Jack Daniels and talking about the music that would be used for forthcoming concert appearances.

## A Driven Personality

Such strong needs fueled his behavior,that he couldn't sit still for long. He was thriving, prospering, going strong, in full swing, feeling like a million, one exuberant self—except when he wasn't at the midpoint of his career. His was a personality that was brimming with infectious energy, enormous confidence, and really big ideas. He thought, talked, moved, and made decisions quickly. He wasn't just a braggart. He was a highly creative person who quickly generated a tremendous number of ideas and projects, mostly clever ones, and then made sure to succeed in them.

There are many personalities who are able to maintain a successful career in business as well as in entertainment who function this way. Clearly, they are blessed with a vigorous, spirited and dynamic temperament.

If there is one trait that distinguishes highly successful people, it is that they are, by temperament, highly motivated and ambitious. "There isn't a minute to waste—this is going to be huge—just do it!" (Gartner, 2005) refers to these people as *hypomanic,* which is seen as a positive trait and is not used as a diagnostic term.

This pressure to act creates overachievers and can in the process lead to impulsive behavior. One outlet for this restless energy has been in business, the excitement of making money and engaging in enterprising projects. Another outlet has been in entertainment, characterized by an elevated mood state that feels highly intoxicating, powerful, productive and desirable to the hypomanic individual. In this state, people are the happiest when they feel creative, energetic, and alive. Another figure in entertainment who fits this image is Sammy Davis Jr., who was always on the "go" in one way or another.

If we drew up a list of their characteristics, it would go something like this. We can see how many of these qualities relate to Sinatra:

- They are filled with energy.
- They are flooded with ideas.
- They are driven, restless, and unable to keep still.
- They channel their energy into the achievement of grand ambitions.
- They often work on little sleep.
- They feel brilliant, special, chosen, and destined to make their mark on the world.
- They can be euphoric.

- They can become easily irritated by minor obstacles.
- They are risk-takers.
- They tend to overspend in both their business and personal lives.
- They act out sexually.
- They are fast-talking.
- They are witty and enormously gregarious.
- Their confidence can make them charismatic and persuasive.
- They are prone to make enemies, and they often feel they are persecuted by those who are critical of their behavior.

In 1956, Sinatra's estimated income for the year was close to a $1 million—an astronomical number in the mid-1950's. There was a crowd at his recording sessions. The atmosphere vibrated with excitement. It wasn't just a record date, it was more of a performance. It was an "in" crowd and it was big and you needed an invitation to get in. It was a "happening" and the air was filled with electricity.

Sinatra's activity level was always high. In 1956 he would travel to Spain to shoot *The Pride and the Passion*; play three, three-week stands at the Sands Hotel while commuting back to L.A. to make records and attend the Motion Picture Awards; sing the "Star-Spangled Banner" at the Democratic National Convention; return to the Paramount Theatre in Times Square to do a week with the Tommy and Jimmy Dorsey Orchestra; and sign a $3 million television contract with ABC and then do some recordings. He went into the recording studio twenty-one times in 1956, the most he had done since 1947. He was just brimming with energy and couldn't stop performing and producing. (Kaplan, 2015)

Feeling strong and powerful does matter. It was the key ingredient in Sinatra's behavior throughout his life. He felt he had to always assert himself like the big guys did or he would be buried. Years later, Sammy Cahn knowingly wrote a song for him (part of the *Robin and the Seven Hoods* score) entitled "I like to Lead when I Dance."

It's really no surprise that early in his career he was drawn to the "Men of Respect," who were often Sicilian like himself, and whom he first encountered in his native Hoboken and Jersey City environs. At the start of his singing career, he discovered that they owned the nightclubs and other venues that presented the kind of entertainment he was involved in. These men were tough, successful, and had unquestioned power. That appealed to the undersized singer with the skinny frame. He wanted success and power, and he wanted them badly.

Throughout his life, Sinatra relished being in the company of "wise guys," enjoying having their power rub off on him. Similarly, they were extremely loyal to him, and over the years he continued to maintain his obligations to them. When things turned especially bad for him in 1951 and 1952, these powerful men kept his career alive.

From the time he left Dorsey, Sinatra became increasingly eager to gain control over his own fortunes. In 1961, Sinatra decided to extend still further the creative freedom and artistic control he had enjoyed throughout most of the 1950's.

He was walking past the Capitol Building in Los Angeles when he turned to a record executive who was accompanying him and said, "I helped build that. Now, let's build one of my own." By the next year, Reprise Records was in business.

His first album, *Ring-a-Ding-Ding*, made a sensational debut, one critic describing it as a "hairy-chested singing."

For his following albums, Sinatra sought out some of the giants of the music industry. While he continued using Billy May, Nelson Riddle, and Gordon Jenkins for their tried-and-true arranging and conducting, he also recorded with Don Costa, Neal Hefti, Sy Oliver, and, most notably, Quincy Jones, who was soon to become a sensation in the entertainment industry. He also recorded three albums with Count Basie and his band and one with the Duke Ellington Orchestra. He did a *bossa nova* album arranged by Claus Ogerman with the composer Antonio Carlos Jobim accompanying him on guitar and voice. The best piece of this period is also the most spontaneous, *Sinatra-Basie Live at the Sands*. This live album presents a picture of someone who really is at the top of his game. In a less muscular vein, Sinatra at age fifty recorded, *September of My Years*, a collection of songs arranged by Jenkins about a man looking back on his life.

His whole life was spectacular, full of action and filled with friends as well a manic thrust forward. Consider following one of his days; he leaves his Palm Springs home early in the morning, which is about noon for him, takes Ringo, his ailing Australian sheep dog, to the vet, boards his six-passenger white and orange Lear Jet, and emerges seventeen minutes later at the Burbank airport. From there he drives his black Dual Ghia to Sinatra Enterprises, a semi-sumptuous bungalow on the Warner Brothers lot, and settles down to work. There is lunch to be had with a visitor. There are songs to be learned and rehearsed with composer Jimmy Van Heusen, a meeting across town at Twentieth Century-Fox, and an evening recording session for his Reprise Records label at a studio on Sunset Boulevard. And this is Sinatra while on vacation.

In addition to his performing chores, his business interests included Artanis Productions, the small organization in which Warner Brothers had the minority holding and Sinatra had the majority holding. Artanis produced the films *None but the Brave*, which Sinatra directed, and *Marriage on the Rocks*, with a new production in preparation. There was also Park Lake Enterprises, a production company outside Warner's bailiwick where he made *4 for Texas, Robin and Seven Hoods* and the phenomenally successful *Von Ryan's Express*.

Cal Jet Airway was a small charter outfit with one Lear, one five-place Alouette helicopter, one three-place Morane-Sanbrier, and another $600,000 Lear on order. Some of his frequent customers were United Artists, Mirisch Brothers, and Paramount; Reprise Records, a company in which Sinatra had a one-third interest and Warner's two thirds; and Titanium Metal Forming Company, which made metal parts for aircraft and missile builders.

He also had extensive acreage in Arizona and California's Marin County, and still owned but did not operate Cal-Neva Lodge at Lake Tahoe, an establishment assessed at $4 million. His license to operate a gambling casino in Nevada was rescinded in 1963 after he had allowed Sam Giancana, a convicted criminal, on the premises, but Sinatra was allowed to operate it.

An additional minor but proud Sinatra holding was an acre of ground in Tennessee, a gift of the Jack Daniels distillery in return for his espousal of the sour mash cause.

By the time that he made his first Clan movie, *Ocean's Eleven*, Sinatra was becoming very rich. He was the boss of a large corporate empire, with stakes in hotels and gambling, movies, music publishing, real estate, and much more. This is both the achievement and power motive in action.

So he was not only busy but also quite wealthy. Educated estimates put his annual gross income at $3 or $4 million. He still got some $60,000 a year in royalties from Columbia Re cords, though he hadn't recorded for them in more than a decade.

Estimates of his personal fortune are quite impressive, and come to around $6 million or $7 million, with $13 million or $14 million as the total worth of Sinatra Enterprises. They were not as gigantic as they could have been, and one reason for this is that he lived like royalty.

For openers, he had three homes: a rented five-room apartment on Manhattan's East River Drive; a ten-room house in Beverly Hills rented from Buddy Adler's widow, Anita Louise; and a home of his very own in Wonder Palms Road, Palm Springs. When he visited Las Vegas, he inhabited the Sands Hotel's Presidential suite.

Only rarely was Sinatra alone. Apart from the many women in his life, he traveled with a sizable retinue of friends, employees, hangers-on, and hangers-on to the hangers. Sinatra's friends had been categorized by the newspapers into packs, clans and sub-clans. To a person, they spoke publicly in almost identical terms of his loyalty and generosity. And they knew the extent of his expansiveness because his activities continued to move out and engulf so many different facets of life. He couldn't stop being extravagant.

Even with his showbiz friends, though, Sinatra remained deep within himself. They felt constrained to keep the talk light. "I don't discuss his girlfriends with Frank or who he's going to marry," said Dean Martin. "All we discuss are movies, TV, golf and drinking."

There is every reason to believe that Sinatra was never the boy next door, not even to the other boys next door in the Hoboken of his youth. He was set apart first by his family's ability to provide well for him in a fairly uncomfortable minority neighborhood, and then by his own relentless determination to make it in the world. The set of qualities that seemed to distinguish Italian-Americans includes individuality, temperament and ambition.

## The Man of Action and Conflict

His popularity was always a worldwide phenomenon. His old records were selling for $33 apiece in the Soviet Union; his films sold out in theatres in Rio; and his status in Japan was almost like a god. Records, picture popularity, personal appearances all reinforced each other.

Power attracts and repels; it functions as an aphrodisiac. Men of power recognize it in others; Sinatra had spent time with Franklin Roosevelt, Jack Kennedy, Richard Nixon, Spiro Agnew, Walter Annenberg, and Ronald Reagan; all wanted his approval, and he wanted and obtained theirs. He could raise millions for them at fundraisers and, in turn, they would always take his calls. On the stage at Caesars Palace, or at an elegant East Side dinner party, Sinatra emanated power. Certainly the dark side of the legend accounts for some of that effect; the myth of the Mafia, after all, is not a myth of evil, but a myth of power.

In 1960, Frank was making millions a year through his film and TV production companies (Essex, Kent, and Dorchester), four music-publishing companies, his gambling interests in Las Vegas and Lake Tahoe, radio partnerships, and his many real estate holdings. The year culminated with Frank's decision to start his own record label, Reprise, even though his contract with Capitol still had two more years to go.

With all of this activity, he had an assignment for *Life* magazine at Madison Square Garden for the Ali v. Frazier "Fight of the Century" on March 8, 1971. In fact Sinatra's photo was used on the magazine's front cover.

His lavish entertaining bespoke not just a man of talent but a man of property. He owned 9 percent of the Sands Hotel in Las Vegas, which he turned almost single-handedly into an entertainment mecca; he became vice-president of the corporation and earned $100,000 for each week he performed, until his falling out with the hotel in 1967. From a time in the sixties, he owned 50 percent of the Cal-Neva Lodge in Lake Tahoe. He also acquired large interests in a small charter airline, a music-publishing house, radio stations, restaurants, and real estate. He formed Essex Productions and received as part of his fee 25 percent of *Pal Joey*. Another Sinatra company received the same percentage for "The Joker is Wild," in which he starred. A button came out at that time with the words. "It's Sinatra's World, We Just Live In It."

## Frank Sinatra: The Swinging Narcissist

He then left Capitol Records because they wouldn't give him a fifty-fifty split, and afterward he formed his own record company, Reprise Records.

Once he received the Academy Award for *From Here to Eternity*, things changed radically for him. He was at the top of *Down Beat's* best male vocalist poll in 1954 after seven years of exile; singer of the year with *Metronome*; No. 1 singer, best album-maker (*Swing Easy*) and best single *(Young at Heart)* with the critics who cast their votes in *Billboard*. These events were the precursor to six years of recording his greatest albums, starring in seventeen films, including the best ones he ever made, roaring around doing concerts and club dates, and together with girlfriends and his gang of male associates, continually making headlines as the carefree, exuberant adult swinger. All of this in addition to pleasing the a large number of people who made up his audience.

The key to his existence now was that he had become essentially his own boss. Remembering the way people and corporations treated him when he was down, he resolved that he would be his own man in the future; he achieved that through a complex agglomeration of private companies which controlled him as he controlled them.

In fashioning Sinatra as a man of action, we could compare him to another man who was a dominant force in music and was as active, hectic and demanding. Leonard Bernstein-was the first superstar conductor to have been born in the USA, a gifted pianist, a fiercely intelligent broadcaster and writer, and an inspiring teacher. On top of all that, he was a composer who wrote successful works both for the concert hall and for Broadway. Add in his complex private life and reckless appetites, and it's no small wonder that at one point he famously described himself as "over-committed on all fronts."

In 1958, he became music director of the Philharmonic, the first American-born musician to hold the post. His eleven seasons in the job transformed him into an icon of the city. Meanwhile, he had established an international career with major orchestras and opera companies all over the world. His worldwide fame was such that, when the Berlin Wall fell in 1989, he was the obvious choice to conduct the celebratory performance there of Beethoven's Ninth Symphony.

Besides a classical music career, Bernstein reached out into the idioms of popular music and jazz. He first came to national attention as a composer of Broadway musicals. His three greatest hits are all set in New York City: *On the Town* (1944), *Wonderful Town,,* (1953), and above all, *West Side Story* (1957). In addition, he wrote the operas *Candide* (1953) and *Trouble in Tahiti* (1951).

While doing this he wrote ballet scores and other symphonic concert pieces. And finally, he wrote a theatre piece for singers, players and dancers. This was called *Mass* (1971). There has never been another composer or conductor who was as active and accomplished as Bernstein. His days were filled with constant musical activity, and that is why he is seen as the most accomplished, talented and manic artist that the music world had ever known. Obviously, the comparison with Sinatra is evident. They were both so driven, intensely ambitious, and with super high achievement and power needs.

## Relationship to His Audience

As with Bernstein, most fans felt an electrical jolt of excitement when Sinatra walked out on the stage. There was an image and personal magnetism and expectation. Part of the art of performance is predicated on the performer's awareness of his audience's expectations and his manipulation of those expectations, either by satisfying them directly or by studied reversal. As Sinatra said, that there is only one way to get the audience with you, and that is to be honest.

*Downbeat,* writing about the hysteria that greeted him, suggested that "his spell is not as artless as it looks. He knows his feminine audience and fires romance-moonlight moods at them with deadly aim."

Sinatra was booked for the second time at the Paramount in 1944. Coming around Columbus Day, this appearance brought the mightiest demonstration of female hysteria that any entertainment star had until then experienced. When Frank arrived the first day for a 6:00 A.M. rehearsal, almost one thousand girls were on line outside. Police estimated that the queue had begun forming at 3:00 A.M. The very first in line had been there since 4:30 P.M. of the preceding day. When the

3600-seat theatre opened its doors at 8:30 A.M., enough youngsters were admitted to fill it to capacity.

The following day, a school holiday, was the haymaker. There was a Columbus Day riot at the theatre. More than 10,000 youngsters queued up in a line six abreast that ran west on Forty-third Street, snaked along Eighth Avenue, and east on Forty-Fourth Street. An additional 20,000 clogged Times Square, making it impassable to pedestrians and automobiles. Prowl cars were summoned by radio from outlying precincts while almost 200 policemen were called from guard duty at the Columbus Day parade on Fifth Avenue. An additional force, including fifty ushers in the theater, could not cope with the frantic crowds. The ticket booth was destroyed in the crush. Shop windows were smashed. When the first show finished, only 250 came out of the 3600-seat house. Most of the youngsters remained glued to their seats for two or three Sinatra appearances.

On the third day, a small riot broke out inside the theater when a stocky eighteen-year-old youth threw an egg at Sinatra. All hell broke loose as security guards pursued the egg thrower, who then was led out of the theater. Sinatra walked off the stage. These unrestrained displays of the bobby-sox brigades were not limited to New York. In Boston, Frank was greeted by 3,000 kids. In Chicago, the windows of his train was shattered and a priest was knocked down and trampled.

Sinatra told the story of a girl who was always in the audience and continually let out a loud yell. Finally, she was told that she could see Sinatra if she would stop that behavior. When she got to see him she promised to stop that screaming if he would give her one of the bowties he wore. He gave her one, and she promised to be quiet. The next day he got out on the stage and there she was, yelling worse than before.

In a long, intellectual article in the *New Republic*, Bruce Bliven said that the bobby-sox reaction, while it may have begun as a publicity stunt, was "a genuine mass phenomenon . . . a phenomenon of mass hysteria." Such hysteria, he explained, was comparable to the Children's Crusade in the Middle Ages, or the dance madness that overwhelmed the young in certain medieval German Villages. To Bliven, the most significant consideration was that Sinatra aligned himself, not only with the younger generation, but also against the adult world. He was thereby rejecting the things that teenagers allegedly hated in the crassly commercial cosmos of their elders, and allowing them to express an unfulfilled hunger for heroes and idealism.

Listening to early recordings of some of Sinatra's songs, one can sense the tremendous tension, mounting emotional anticipation, and demand for release that the delayed fondling of words and notes engendered. It required only a twist of the head, a glimmer of a smile, to provoke a young audience that was turned on by the suspenseful sound of his voice. His singing was never merely an entertainment, but an experience to which audiences felt compelled to respond, not only with applause, but with their hearts. From the start of his solo career, he was an involved singer who forced involvement upon his listeners. His singing expressed a feeling of intimacy, the intense personalization of lyrics, and the glow of sheer sex.

Sinatra was skilled at giving each of his listeners the impression that they was the particular inspiration of, and target for, the sentiments he was proclaiming. While singing to an audience, he rarely gazed abstractedly into space. Instead, he stared with shattering intensity into the eyes of one trembling disciple after another. Sinatra handled his kids, as he calls them, with artful skill. One theatrical agent mentioned, "I never saw anything like the way he milks 'em and kids 'em around."

Sinatra had two thousand fan clubs that were insatiable. In the first generation, Sinatra sang to the people, from whom he learned that, from cradle to grave, people love to be sung to. They first heard him when he sang with Dorsey, and when, in the last falsetto note of "The Song is You," he seemed oddly and engagingly close to internal explosion. Then they heard a new Sinatra, free of the insistent big-band beat, singing simple ballads, eloquently:

The smile of Turner and the scent of roses
The waiters whistling as the last bar closes.

Brad Dexter put it this way: "He has an insatiable desire to live every moment to its fullest because, I guess, he feels that right around the corner is extinction."

In 1945, the 29-year-old Sinatra came to Hollywood, and immersed himself in the Hollywood social scene. He was thrilled to live in California and anxious to fit in; he became friendly with many of the town's most influential popular entertainers, such as Lauren Bacall and Humphrey Bogart, Jack Benny and Bing Crosby, who were more than happy to welcome him into their ranks. He also attracted women like Lana Turner and Marilyn Maxwell, who were interested in him. He had grown within a few short years from a lovelorn microphone-hugging crooner into one of filmdom's leading and most vocal battlers for a democratic way of life. But he could never turn away from where the action was.

## Other Musicians, Arrangers and Song Writers

Mutual respect and understanding brought Sinatra and Axel Stordahl together in the early forties to develop their working relationship into one of the first true musical partnerships of the pop-music era. The sumptuous string arrangements Stordahl made for Sinatra became synonymous with the suave, romantic image that enveloped him as the premiere "crooner" of the 1940s. Simplicity was the key to their beauty and understated sonority.

The famed "Columbia sound" was achieved through the employment of the very best engineers, custom-designed equipment, and the finest recording facilities—all skillfully coordinated under the watchful eye of label chief Goddard Lieberson. And then Sinatra met such greats as Nelson Riddle, Billy May, and Gordon Jenkins. All these fine arrangers would help to produce the thematically unified albums that were to become Sinatra trademarks; they were the best in the business and he would only use the best—his achievement needs were so high.

As a man of action, someone always on the move, Sinatra wanted arrangers who could propel and enhance his image. When considering his studio recordings of the fifties, we must distinguish between the contributions of these three brilliant arrangers: Nelson Riddle, Billy May, and Gordon Jenkins. Each orchestrated and conducted several albums with

Sinatra at Capitol Records, and their very different approaches provide another clear index to the disjunctive nature of Sinatra's singing persona. Billy May tended to write driving, brassy big-band arrangements, usually without strings, full of humor and extroverted energy. He's best known for the songs "Come Fly with Me," "Come Dance with Me" and "Come Swing with Me," whose titles suggest an open and gregarious stance toward their audience. Gordon Jenkins wrote lush, brooding string arrangements for two crucial ballad albums of the fifties—*Where are You?* and *No One Cares*, records that plumb the depths of introversion and erotic suffering. Sinatra once said that Jenkins' arrangements show a kinship with Bernard Herrmann's score for Hitchcock's *Vertigo*, arguably one of the greatest films of the fifties and a work that explores much the same region of obsessive eros and loss mapped by Sinatra's ballad albums.

Riddle was a trombonist-arranger who had recorded with Nat Cole, Les Baxter, and others. His first work with Sinatra involved some Billy May sound-alikes, such as "South of the Border," but also included arrangements that were uniquely his, such as "I've Got the World on a String" and "Don't Worry 'Bout Me." Riddle's ability to build a song to a peak meshed with Sinatra's passion for lyrics, and both found their format in the newly developed long-playing record, which permitted endless storytelling. Riddle noted, "In working out an arrangement, I look for the peak of a song and build to it. We're telling a story. It has to have a beginning, a middle, a climax and an ending."

As a result of Riddle's musical conceptions, Sinatra's recordings really began to swing during this period, which can best be appreciated on the recordings labeled the "swinging ballads." Sinatra's sensual reading and Riddle's pulsating arrangement managed to achieve great romantic tensions while swinging all the way—a neat feat. Nelson Riddle developed a style that could bridge the gap between the swinger and the loser, allowing the singer to move between them convincingly in the course of the album and even within individual songs. Sinatra did his finest work with Riddle precisely because Riddle's arrangements helped him to articulate the relationship between inside and outside so fully.

While May worked only on swing albums and Jenkins on ballad albums, Riddle did both, including the two *masterpieces* of Sinatra's

Capitol period, *Songs for Swingin' Lovers* and *Only the Lonely*. More to the point, Riddle learned to integrate the two modes and to play them against one another on a very fine level. Under Sinatra's guidance, he created what's come to be called the "swing ballad" idiom, fusing operatic expressiveness and rhythmic drive. With its inner tensions and clashing colors, this style proved the perfect vehicle for Sinatra's exploration of the more slippery areas of his vocal self.

Riddle complemented Sinatra's talents better than anyone else. Whereas Sinatra could rely on Stordahl and Gordon Jenkins to pen wistful orchestrations that spoke tenderly of love and youth and spring, and Billy May to sound all the whistles and bells with his full-steam-ahead tempo charts, it was Nelson Riddle and his unflappable temperament who provided an even keel. From their first studio session on April 30, 1953, the duo carefully crafted and perfected such an extraordinary signature sound that Riddle became sought after by dozens of other famous vocalists wishing to duplicate the immensely successful Sinatra-Riddle style for their own recordings. With the first song they tackled on that momentous occasion, the dynamic and explosive "I've Got the World on a String," the tone was set. It was obvious that the pair were of one musical mind and that their perspectives had quickly melded into a totally cohesive and effective whole to produce incredibly tight and polished performances. The style that Riddle developed and perfected for Sinatra went far beyond the arrangements he was doing for Nat King Cole and Judy Garland, which were very special in their own right. Riddle had said that Sinatra brought out his best work and that "He's stimulating to work with. You have to be right on your mettle all the time. The man himself somehow draws everything out of you" (Douglas-Home, p. 33).

While he was busy perfecting his vocal art, he was equally busy in front of the movie cameras. As mentioned previously, during the Capitol years, he made such films as *From Here to Eternity, Suddenly, Young at Heart, The Tender Trap, Guys and Dolls, The Man with the Golden Arm, Johnny Concho, High Society, The Joker is Wild, Pal Joey, Some Came Running, A Hole in the Head, The Manchurian Candidate,* and *Come Blow Your Horn*. His performances ranged from dreadful to outstanding while he became a major film box-office attraction.

Although he emerged in the 1950's as a major movie star, it was his singing at this time that elevated both his own stature and that of the American popular song. He may have been a phenomenon in the 1940's, but he was now a very serious singer who carefully chose his material. He revolutionized his art by taking the American song and laying it out before the world in a way that exposed the melody, the lyrics, and the feelings associated with each song. This was certainly the achievement motive in action.

## SINATRA'S CONCERTS

Many of Sinatra's concerts and tours, including "The Main Event" (1974), "The Concert for the Americas" (Dominican Republic, 1982), "The Ultimate Event" (1988), and "The Diamond Jubilee World Tour" (1991), were promoted as extravaganzas. These extravagant titles, which do not presage the entrance of a humble artist, were well earned by the singer, not only for his superb performances, but also for his sheer drawing power. A single 1980 concert in Brazil attracted an audience of 175,000— a number that, at the time, qualified as a Guinness world record for a solo performer.

## COLLABORATORS AND SONGWRITERS

Just as there are clues to the essential Sinatra in his early music, these are present also in his choice of collaborators. Certainly he knew how to find out who was writing the good songs of the day, and among Jule Styne, Sammy Cahn, and Jimmy Van Heusen, not one had yet made a reputation of any size before hooking up with Sinatra.

Prior to his first solo decade, Sinatra gained valuable insight during his tenure as the band vocalist with both James (1939) and Dorsey (1940-1942). It was during these gigs that he befriended many of the talented musicians who would weave their way into the very fabric of his musical existence: Sammy Cahn, arranger Axel Stordahl, and musician Skitch Henderson among them. Then, too, came the first inkling of his discriminating taste for top-quality songs, and his knack for selecting only those tunes that he instinctively knew fit his style like a fine leather glove. As far back as the early 1940's, Sinatra credited Tommy Dorsey with providing the rudimentary elements that he would adapt to fit his vocal styling, carefully refining his approach to develop a distinct method of phrasing that would become unmistakably his own.

When Sinatra was signed to do *Anchors Aweigh,* he said to the producers that he wanted Sammy Cahn to write the score. They were a bit resistant because they hadn't heard of Cahn, but he said to them: "Since you aren't doing the singing and I am, let me be the judge of who writes the words I sing." Yet some time later they had a real falling-out. Someone told Sinatra that at a dinner party his name had been taken in vain. Sinatra thought that Cahn should have slapped the offending person's face. Cahn knew that he couldn't do that, nor did he think it was that serious. But when Frank heard about it, he didn't speak to Cahn for about a year. Then after a year, Cahn received a phone call from him.

Cahn was in Palm Springs when the phone rang and Frank was on the other line. Cahn just said, "Hi, how're you doing?"

"Pretty good."

"I'd been hoping you were great. I've been reading that you're going into the Copacabana."

Frank said, "That's what I'm calling you about. I need some songs."
I said I had three or four ideas: I'd write them and mail them to him.
He sent the material to Sinatra and thought that would end the matter.
However, the phone rang again.
The stuff was marvelous and would I please come to New York.
I said, "Frank, you don't need me, it's all there. Just do it."
"Please come to New York. Please . . ."
These were the days before the planes. I took the *Twentieth Century Limited,* arriving at Grand Central at eight in the morning. Frank was at the Hampshire House. I rushed to the hotel at eight-thirty, only to be informed that Mr. Sinatra had left a note saying he was not to be disturbed until one o'clock.

So Sammy waited and then came back later to confront him. He told Frank:

"I want to talk to you. You and I haven't talked in over a year. Maybe we won't ever talk again, but you must hear what I have to say. For a year

## The Man of Action and Conflict

now I've agonized over your inactivity. You're not number one. I've seen every second-rate singer pass you. If I called a music publisher and said, 'Do you have a number for Frank Sinatra,' they'd hang up on me. Frank I'm doing very well—I'm making $100,000 a year—but I'll quit what I am doing and stay with you. And we both know I'm not being altruistic, because if you do what you're capable of I'll make twenty times that."

He kept saying, "I know, I know . . ."

Afterward, Cahn took the train back to California. Later when Frank was going into the Empire Room of the Waldorf he called again. Sammy went over to see him and laid out his act, starting with "They've Got an Awful Lot of Coffee in Brazil."

Cahn mentions that he is not a sycophant or masochist, and he said that he never ran with Sinatra. "I'm certainly not knocking the ones who have and do, but for me it's all a bit too much; it tends to take over too much of your life, too much of the phone ringing and a voice saying, "Now hear this, Frank wants . . ." Frank didn't expect it from him. but then Cahn says that he is attracted to dynamic, talented people, and Frank Sinatra more than qualified on both counts. He would sum up Sinatra in this way: "He has been the ultimate dream."

He never burned out, and the fact he kept going was, to his audience, a reaffirmation of themselves. Sinatra was magic to those who came of age in the 1940's. His art— the unmatched phrasing and breath control; the emotional readings of American popular song; his work with the finest arrangers, conductors, and musicians in the country; and the untiring musical perfectionism— has left an indelible mark on the American Song Book.

John Rockwell, commenting on one of Sinatra's recording sessions, said, "What makes Sinatra so marvelous this late in life in his unflagging commitment to his craft and art. He never gave up, never let even the silliest material overcome his sense of style, never (for long, at least) allowed the routine of performance or the indulgences of vast wealth to dull his desire to do the very best he could." (Rockwell, 1985, p, 231).

While he would work with dozens of talented individuals throughout the sixty-year span of his career, he remained loyal to a relatively small group of arrangers, who used his boundless musical energy and insight as a springboard for creating not only his orchestrations (which were usually far superior to any they wrote for other singers), but as the inspiration for their own personal work as well.

To appreciate fully why he and the arrangers were so effective in bringing their tremendous forces together in the studio, we must first assess the underlying foundation of their musical partnerships and how intense pre-studio planning had, in the end, just as much of a hand in the outcome as the actual sessions. An in-depth look at the Sinatra-Riddle "marriage" serves to illustrate the optimal relationship between vocalists and arrangers and the often-inexplicable factors that combine to produce music of uncommon beauty.

Sinatra felt that Riddle was the greatest arranger in the world, that there such a great depth to the music he created. "If I say, 'Make like Puccini,' Nelson will make exactly the same little note, and that eighth bar will be Puccini all right, and the roof will lift off!" (Douglas-Home, p.) 35).

Through the years, Sinatra worked only with orchestrators or arrangers who could interpret the music his way: Axel Stordahl, Nelson Riddle, and other giants in that field like Billy May, Gordon Jenkins, Johnny Mandel, Neal Hefti, George Siravo, Robert Farnon, and Don Costa. Sinatra knew which orchestrator worked best on which kind of song, and so he selected songs with the orchestrator in mind.

Gordon Jenkins once said that he would never question Frank's ideas, because "I've never seen him wrong. Every suggestion that he's ever made to me has been an improvement."

## CONNECTIONS WITH THE UNDERWORLD

In 1947 Sinatra was asked by Joe Fischetti, a buddy he had known from Hoboken since 1938, if he would like to meet Lucky Luciano, the boss of the Cosa Nostra crime syndicate. Luciano had been in exile in Havana since late October, 1946, and was living a good life in a spacious estate in the exclusive Miramar surburb.

At this time, Luciano was planning the first full-scale confab for American underworld leaders since a Chicago gathering in 1932, which would be held on the upper floors of the Hotel Nacional in Havana, a busy mecca for gamblers. Luciano wanted it to be known that he would be the boss of bosses. At the beginning of 1947, the delegates – all known by the FBI to be members of the syndicate and recognized gangsters – began to show up in Havana for this conference of big shots. Frank Costello, Augie Pisano, Mike Miranda, Joe Adonis, Tommy "Three Fingers" Brown Lucchese, Joe Profaci, Willie Moretti, Albert Anastasia and Joe "Bananas" Bonanno arrived from New York and New Jersey. Others came from different cities.

As soon as each arrived they would first go to Luciano's villa and pay homage to him, and then each would give him an envelope stuffed with cash - $150,000 in all – which Luciano used to buy points in the casino at the Nacional. Then they would retire to a suite that was reserved for them and wait for Luciano to join them.

Fischetti had proposed to Frank that Frank and Nancy meet him in Miami for a February vacation, after which Frank and Joe, Charlie and Rocky Fischetti would go to Havana and meet Lucky Luciano. Frank couldn't wait to go. In his old Hoboken neighborhood, thugs like Luciano were revered by the underdogs of the neighborhood, the Italians. He wanted to know someone as important as Luciano, to be in his company, and to socialize with such a dangerous character.

However, Frank did not realize that he would be used as a cover for the conference in order to give it an air of legitimacy. Frank thought he was going to Havana just to meet Luciano, but unbeknownst to him, Luciano was telling people that his friends from across the country were coming to Havana to meet Sinatra. Notice how the most extreme of his power needs emerged with this opportunity.

On February 11, Frank and the Fischettis flew to Havana and checked into the Hotel Nacional. In a few days, Frank came to the startling realization that he was surrounded by a bunch of known criminals, all of whom wanted his autograph. Although he was frightened at first, he realized he couldn't just leave. It wouldn't look good, so he decided to stay and have a good time. He gambled at the casino, went to the races and to a party with Luciano, and never gave a second thought to how all of this would appear to his public and to his critics when his presence in Havana became known.

## Frank Sinatra: The Swinging Narcissist

A confidante of Luciano confided: "Frank was a good kid and we was all proud of him, the way he made it to the top . . . a skinny kid from around Hoboken with a terrific voice and one hundred percent Italian. He used to sing around the joints there, and all the guys liked him."

When the time came when some dough was needed to put Frank across with the public, they put it up. He was only making about a hundred and fifty dollars with Tommy Dorsey and he needed publicity, clothes, different kinds of special things for his music, and they all cost quite a bit of money, maybe in the range of fifty or sixty grand. They fronted the money, it all helped him become a big star, and he was just "showin' his appreciation by comin' down to Havana and sayin' hello to me," as Luciano said. But the story never made sense. Sinatra never needed that kind of money and he probably would not have accepted it from them at that time. It sounded as if Sinatra wanted to rub shoulders with these big names, even if they did come from the underworld.

However, when his manager George Evans learned about Sinatra's whereabouts, he couldn't believe it and almost had a heart attack. He flew to where Sinatra was and confronted him, but Sinatra held his ground and told him, "Look, I'm playing with the big boys down here. Don't ruin it for me. I ain't doing nothing but having fun."

There were rumors that Sinatra carried a suitcase containing $2 million to give to Luciano, but that was easily discounted. A week later Luciano was arrested by Cuban officials for a crime he did not commit and then sent back to Italy. Many years later, in 1972, a troop of police raided Luciano's penthouse in Rome and seized some of his belongings. A gold lighter was later found among his possessions, inscribed, "To my dear pal, Charlie, from his friend, Frank Sinatra." This kind of story would add to Sinatra's career because it made him appear to be a dangerous guy. There seemed to be an aura of excitement around him associated with the lives of gangsters. (Kaplan, 2005)

As mentioned in Chapter Four, Sinatra made his work and life itself resemble a game, with variety, appropriate flexible challenges, clear goals, and immediate feedback. The quality of his life depended on two factors: how he experienced work and his relations with other people. He was most happy when he was in the company of friends because friendships allowed him to express parts of his being that he seldom had the opportunity to act out otherwise. Taking part in the Rat Pack allowed him to express a part of himself that gave him great enjoyment, as well as widening his life into the realms of politics, business, and mob-related friendships.

Another way of understanding how we order our actions is to focus on the complexity of the challenges we set for ourselves, rather than on the content itself. What matters is how differentiated and integrated are the goals that we pursue and how well-related these traits are to each other. In that respect, a well-thought-out-feelings approach to life, one that is responsive to a great variety of concrete human experiences and is internally consistent, is preferable to an unreflective optimism.

## COMPOSITE MIND

When you look at Sinatra, you see such opposing forces existing within him. He could be tender and rough, vulnerable and domineering, boundlessly charitable and infinitely rancorous, a lover of string quartets and an admirer of mobsters, the most serious of artists and a childish prankster, perfectionistic while recording songs and yet impatient on a movie set. The contradictions that constantly were embedded in his mind make him a personality that defied comprehension. It was never clear where the center existed. Sammy Cahn, his close lyricist for many years, commented, "There isn't any 'real' Sinatra. There's only what you see . . . There's nothing inside him. He puts out so terrifically that nothing can accumulate inside."

It would be exhausting to follow Sinatra's life year by year, sometimes day by day or even hour by hour. He had such a large amount of relentless energy that he had few instances of downtime. Albums he did with Nelson Riddle include *In the Wee Small Hours (1955), Songs for Swingin' Lovers! (1956),* and *Only the Lonely (1958).* He demonstrated his great natural acting abilities in films such as *Suddenly (1954), The Man with the Golden Arm (1955), and Some Came Running (1958).* And he took his place as the ultimate headliner at the Sands in Las Vegas, the Fontainebleau in Miami, the Copa in New York. These achievements were more than matched by an offstage life in which sex, Jack Daniels, and boisterous all-night partying kept him from ever feeling fatally unoccupied. "So long as I keep busy, I feel great," he told a reporter in 1956.

He was a central player in all the avenues of power, so that political and media power, star power, sexual power, and mob power were all mixed together. And yet he was able to pull it off with much success except on rare occasions. As mentioned previously, a high point for Sinatra was reached when he organized Kennedy's inaugural gala, a three-hour stage spectacle featuring such disparate talents as Gene Kelly, Eleanor Roosevelt, Laurence Olivier, Ella Fitzgerald, Joey Bishop, Nat King Cole, and Leonard Bernstein. And the sweetest moment came to Sinatra when he heard these words tripping off Kennedy's tongue: "I know we're all indebted to a great friend, Frank Sinatra... Long after he has ceased to sing, he is going to be standing up and speaking for the Democratic Party, and I thank him on behalf of all of you tonight."

Sinatra would play these words over and over again, and he made his friends listen to it also. His daughter Tina had noted, "Had he been a healthier, less tortured man, he might have been Perry Como."

CHAPTER SEVEN

# His Legacy

## What is a Legacy?

Sharing conversation over beers with a group of friends, a 30-something young male proclaimed that this was his last summer of singlehood, because he was planning to get married in the fall and wanted to start a family immediately. More typically it is the female in her late thirties who feels the urgency of her biological clock ticking and is eager to settle into family life; so he was asked, why?

"I want to leave a legacy," he answered. It seemed that he was following a checklist of Middle-American conformist ideals of what must be accomplished to attain a successful life. Yet, following his rather lopsided and naïve answer, he began to defend himself.

"Seriously!" someone snapped. "How can you think your offspring are your gift or possession?"

"A legacy," he continued, "is what *you* leave behind when your physical being has passed on."

A legacy is the lessons that we learn from someone's life, the meaning of their lives, their struggles, their work ethic, their loves— as well as their friendships and family, the way they lived and constructed their lives, and what significance these lives for future generations after they have passed on.

Some call it *karma* or the results of one's actions. For an artist, it is his or her art; for a writer, it is the words; for a musician, it is music; for an entrepreneur, it is a business invention; for a gardener, it is a beautiful landscape; for a chef, it is a new recipe.

By legacy, then, we mean the insights people leave that have resonance for the lives they touched, both professional and personal. What has that person left that enables others to understand the inner workings of their behavior and their mind? A person who has made such a huge impact and mark on their world must have left much wisdom and many truths that can be shared with future generations.

In 1939, Sinatra started on the road to stardom when he became the lead singer for Harry James, and from thereon his trajectory continued to soar. Once he had a foothold into the world of entertainment he would then ascend to the pinnacle of success. He took the world by storm. In the same year, another dominating personality started on his path toward success. In future years, he also became a legend and was considered one in a million and the most gifted hitter of his time. His name was Ted Williams and he was nicknamed "the kid." In the public imagination, Williams was almost a god among men, a "superhuman" endowed with a collection of innate physical gifts, spectacular eye-hand coordination, exquisite muscular grace, and uncanny instincts.

As a boy, Williams wasn't interested in passively watching his natural abilities unfold like a flower in the sunshine. He simply wanted and needed to be the best hitter that baseball had ever seen, and he pursued that goal with ferocity. "His whole life was hitting the ball," recalled a childhood friend. "He always had that bat in his hand . . . And when he made up his mind to do something, he was going to do it or know the reason why."

Friends who lived near Williams recalled his hitting baseballs every waking hour of every day, year after year. They described him slugging balls until their outer shells literally wore off, swinging even splintered bats for hours upon hours with blisters on his fingers and blood dripping down his wrists. From ages six to seven, he would swing that bat at North Parkfield all day and night, until the city turned off the lights; then he'd walk home and swing a roll of newspaper in front of a mirror until he fell asleep. He said on many occasions that he wasn't going to let anything stop him from being the hitter he hoped to be.

## His Legacy

He worked for it, fiercely, single-mindedly, far beyond the norm. Greatness was not a thing to Ted Williams; it was a process. When he became a pro he continued to discuss the science of hitting *ad nauseam* with teammates and opposing players. He sought out the great hitters of the game and grilled them about their techniques. He also studied pitchers with the same rigor and wanted to figure them out. In short, Williams knew what he had to do to become one of the best hitters of all time.

After a decade of relentless effort on North Park field and four impressive years in the minors, Williams came into the major leagues in 1939 as an explosive hitter, and just kept getting better and better. In 1941, the same year that Sinatra made such impressive hit records with Tommy Dorsey, Williams, then in his third year with the Boston Red Sox, became the only major league player in his era and in the twentieth century to bat over .400 for a full season.

But, technically, this was not the last time Williams hit .400. It was not even the highest batting average of his career. Williams had left baseball to serve in the military in Korea on August 6, so he had only 110 plate appearances for the season. Williams' rapid return to greatness remains the high mark for a player returning after an extended absence.

At the time of his return, Williams was 34, but clearly still in his prime. He had missed all but the first six games of the 1952 season as well (he hit .400 in those six games), but in the full seasons on either end of his military service, he led the American League in on-base and slugging percentages, and he continued as a highly productive player until his retirement in 1960, hitting a home run in his final at-bat at 42. His comeback and resumption of a brilliant career overlaps with Sinatra's comeback and stardom in *From Here to Eternity*.

The single greatest lesson from studying the lives of both Sinatra and Williams is not how easily things came to them, but how irrepressible and resilient they were. That they wanted to succeed, wanted it so badly that they would never give up, so badly that they were ready to sacrifice time, money, sleep, friendships, and to adopt a particular lifestyle of ambition, not just for a few weeks or months but for years and years. Uncommon achievement requires an uncommon level of personal motivation and a massive amount of faith.

As Nietzsche said, "All great artists and thinkers are great workers, indefatigable not only in inventing, but also in rejecting, sifting, transforming, ordering." And super-achievers of whatever age are dreamers. They must have part of their heads stuck in the clouds in order to imagine the unimaginable. They have to ignore their obvious shortcomings and what may often look like immovable obstacles. To defer to the impediments would amount to instant defeat. The true road to success lies in developing the most productive attitude and identifying magnificent external resources.

Looking at Sinatra and Williams, it is clear that both had exceptional drive. For both, that kind of obsessive ambition appeared around the same time, in adolescence. Intense ambition evolves out of complex, real-world dynamics, settling into people's psyches at different ages and circumstances—sometimes as a result of extreme adversity, sometimes as a proxy for revenge, sometimes as a way of proving oneself to a feared parent or sibling. The collection of potential catalysts for intense ambition may never be entirely understood and will surely never be easily reproduced. But it still may be important to try and understand the dynamic.

Looking at Sinatra and Ted Williams and also at Michael Jordan, a similar process may be evident. Jordan always seemed to hate losing but his drive to improve his skills didn't appear until his rejection from the varsity squad in tenth grade. Afterward, according to friends, he went into overdrive. A competitive streak became evident and he practiced and played as hard as he could. "All top athletes are driven," writes journalist David Halberstam, "and no one made the University of North Carolina roster unless he was by far the hardest-working kid in his neighborhood, his high school and finally his high school conference, but Jordan was self-evidently the most driven of all."

In fact, Jordan impressed his coach with his extra level of ferocity and he seemed to get more intense with each passing year. Jordan was constantly working on the weaker part of his game trying to bring it up. As with the others, it was his desire to be the best. After his junior year, coach Smith realized there was nothing else he could do for him, and he pushed Jordan to leave college ball for the NBA.

## His Legacy

One common characteristic that all three of these men shared was that at some point in their lives, they came to realize how much the process of improvement was within their own control. People who believe that their talents are malleable and can be increased through hard work are much more ambitious and successful. They believe that what they have can only be improved with hard work.

Sinatra's personal vision, motivation, and belief in himself developed him into a resilient character and made him such a celebrated figure. Having such a vision does not excuse a man for some of his failings. However, this drive kept him awake until the wee small hours and fueled the charisma that made him *Sinatra*.

As far as he was concerned, the boy next door matured into the man whose commerce with his vision made him more poignantly wistful, more intensely passionate, and more deeply brokenhearted than the usual person.

It was not only his drive that led to his success, but also fortunate timing. To take another example, the popularity of both Frank Sinatra and Elvis Presley was not an accident, but a logical product of the intersection of mass media with an audience yearning for something to claim as its own. No matter how distinctive their styles and important their contribution to the history of American music, these two performers became popular because they gave their audiences exactly what they wanted. No matter how singular their personalities, they mirror, at least in their origins, classic American self-made men. Both Sinatra and Presley gained notoriety by virtue of their appeal to the youthful audiences of their respective eras.

Sinatra and Elvis represented something with which their teenage fans could identify with, and their success would come to represent a twentieth-century version of Horatio Alger's mythology that hard work and ambition and steadfast dedication lead to material success and public recognition. What sustains the Alger hero, above all, is his determination and desire to succeed. Combining his hard work, conspicuous moral character, deferential respect, and concern for others with an adventurous spirit, this desire enables the hero to take advantage of the lucky breaks that come his way, to merit the confidence of his mentors, and to emerge triumphant. And when success is finally his, the Alger hero appropriately does not forget his humble origins, for he is scrupulous about repaying debts, sharing his rewards with those less fortunate, and caring lavishly for those who depend upon him.

Both Sinatra and Presley were no strangers to hard times and personal struggles, and although the urban ethnic enclaves of Hoboken stand in sharp contrast to the rural hard scrabble of Tupelo and the segregated southern gumbo of Memphis, the two families shared common experiences.

It seems a bit odd that when Sinatra was asked what he thought of Presley, he condemned the new musical phenomenon. In a magazine article, he decried rock and roll as "brutal, ugly, degenerate, vicious... It fosters almost totally negative and destructive reactions in young people. It smells phony and false. It is sung, played and written, for the most part, by cretinous goons... This rancid-smelling aphrodisiac I deplore." Asked for a response, Presley said, "I admire the man. He has a right to say what he wants to say. He is a great success and a fine actor, but I think he shouldn't have said it . . . This is a trend, just the same as he faced when he started years ago." But, Sinatra never had much trouble with saying whatever he felt at that moment.

What is also odd is that when Presley came out of the Army, Sinatra quickly signed him to his show and they sang a few songs together, Presley singing Sinatra's material and Sinatra singing some of the songs that made Presley popular. We can see here Sinatra's relentless drive to succeed, since he didn't care for Presley's songs but he knew he was immensely popular and would bump up the ratings for his show.

In the 1940s, songwriter Sammy Cahn had this to say about Frank: "I'd never heard a popular singer with such fluidity and style." By then he had become the top male vocalist of the year in *Billboard* Magazine and a favorite of the teenage audience. Dorsey told a reporter, "You could almost feel the excitement coming up out of the crowds, when that kid stood up to sing . . . I used to stand there so amazed that I'd almost forget to take my own solos." When Frank decided to break from the Dorsey band in 1942, the move heralded a new direction not only for him but for the male vocalist as performer. No longer content to be just another instrument in the band, Frank felt that he should be the center of the attention that already seemed to be directed his way, and in a few months after his final performance with Dorsey, he would come to witness the magnitude of that attention.

In an April 1965 *Life* Magazine article, Frank Sinatra wrote, "Of the male newcomers, Jack Jones is the best potential singer in the business. He has a distinction, an all-around quality, that puts him potentially about three lengths in front of the other guys." Unfortunately, the combination of a lack of drive, the wrong attitude, and the difficulties involved in trying to overcome the onslaught of rock 'n' roll, eventually stymied the growth of Jones' career. Yet this statement shows how perceptive Sinatra was when it came to sizing up another singer's performance.

Frank then went on to say that Tommy was a good teacher because he had a great band, he had wonderful vocalists with him, and they were great together. "But without Tommy I know it still would have happened ... Frank had a master plan for himself, and he worked at getting there. I think he always had it in the back of his mind that this was a stepping stone." (Levinson, Tommy Dorsey, p. 155)

In order to establish himself as a solo performer, it was important for Sinatra to seek out an important agent at a major talent agency to represent him. He found him in Frank Cooper, the head of the radio department at General Amusement Corporation (GAC), which had formerly been Rockwell-O'Keefe.

At ninety-three, the outgoing and still very involved agent Cooper remembered, "I had met Frank when he was with Harry James. I used to visit him then and afterward when he went with Dorsey ... I got pretty close to him. We got to talking about his leaving the band. After he told Dorsey he wanted to leave, he called me and I said, 'Frank, go to work.' The guys at GAC thought I was crazy. They didn't think Frank was going to make it. I thought he was a poet."

When Sinatra got back to New York, he told Cooper that he had made a deal with Dorsey and Leonard Vannerson releasing him from his contract. Cooper was shocked, and asked to see it. Cooper recalled:

> He showed me the papers and then I saw that he gave Tommy Dorsey 33 1/3 percent of his gross earnings and 10 percent to

Vannerson to do this! 'This is crazy. You'll be broke all your life because there's a thing called income taxes on top of that!' And so he said to me, 'I wanted to get out of that!' Then he had to pay 10 percent more to us as his agent! I said, 'We can't get out of that.' 'Don't worry,' he said, 'I'm not paying him a quarter. He can do whatever he pleases.'

However, there was another story that was told about this incident. Frank may have used his Mob allies to get him out of the hefty penalty that he faced for breaking his contract with Tommy. According to Tommy, Willie Moretti and two other associates paid him a visit, letting Tommy know the lethal consequences of failing to back down. Tommy reported that he took the hint and settled the contract with Frank. Frank's release from the contract terms made him known in the federal law enforcement world as a mob collaborator.

## FLOW

Very little has been written about the elements behind the tenacity that Sinatra had in approaching his music. He loved singing and could sing at the drop of a hat. There was nothing that afforded him more excitement. He worked at it until the last days of his life as if nothing else mattered as much to him. Mihaly Csikszentmihalyi has developed a theory of the good life based on his idea of "flow." This is the state in which people are so involved in an activity that nothing else seems to matter; the experience itself is so enjoyable and stimulating that people will do it even at great cost, for the sheer sake of doing it. And they will continue doing it endlessly because it gives them so much pleasure. It would seem that all artists must have this, or else they would not be able to devote so much time and energy to their rehearsing as well as to their artistic creations.

By stretching our skills and reaching toward greater challenges, we lose all consideration of time, and we become completely absorbed in what we are doing. Certainly writers have this, as well as athletes and different kinds of performers.

## His Legacy

If we look at Sinatra's behavior throughout his professional life at recording sessions or performances, we see many of the qualities described as "flow." The concern for the self disappears as one becomes deeply immersed in the task at hand. Much of this can be seen in musicians who can practice for hours and yet it feels to them as if little time had elapsed. The sense of duration is so altered that hours seem to pass by in minutes.

In an interview with Jerry Seinfeld (*New York Times*, 09/15/02), he talks about how he spends his time since he stopped doing his television show. He says that he wanders around his neighborhood on the Upper West Side "people-watching, sliding in and out of shops, pausing perhaps on a park bench or two and taking in what he sees and whether something in it might provide the seed for a good stand-up routine."

Jerry goes on to tell the interviewer, Rick Lyman, how important it is to motivate yourself with challenges. "That's how you know you're alive. Once you start doing only what you've already proven you can do, you're on the road to death." This is a good way of differentiating Sinatra from many of his rival crooners.

Seinfeld recounted a time when he was working in Boston in 1993. He started doing this routine and someone out in the audience yelled, "Heard it!" He felt as if someone threw a spear from the balcony and it went right through his chest.

Walking out on stage and approaching an audience creates an opportunity to act in a special kind of world, a world of record and legend and cherished significance. But the performer needs to be unique and fresh with his material. Once the celebrity accepts this position in life he is no longer living his own life. Others are living in him, by him, with him. They may dislike him or love him or berate him, or even glory in him. He has given up his private image and assumed a worldly persona. That is, he is now a representative of others and his actions are vicariously theirs. His sufferings and his triumphs, his failures and his courage, his good fortune and his ill fortune, all become theirs. If the fates favor him, they also favor them. His deeds become messages from beyond, as if some saint has interceded. Only by such an interpretation can we explain the dynamics of the psychic bond between a performer and the fans.

Although the flow experience appears to be effortless, it is far from being so. It often involves highly disciplined mental activity and the application of a skilled performance. While it lasts, consciousness works smoothly, and action follows action seamlessly.

And, of course, feedback is important. Some people are born with exceptional sensitivity to sound. They can discriminate among different tones and pitches, and recognize and remember combinations of sounds better than the general population. It is likely that such individuals will be attracted to playing with sounds; they will learn to control and shape auditory information. Composers, singers, performers, conductors, and even music critics will develop from among them. One of the most frequently mentioned dimensions of the flow experience is that, while it lasts, one is able to forget all the unpleasant aspects of life. The feature of flow is an important by-product of the fact that enjoyable activities require a complete focusing of attention on the task at hand—thus leaving no room in the mind for irrelevant information. When an activity is thoroughly engrossing, there is not enough attention left over to allow a person to consider either the past or the future, or any other temporarily irrelevant stimuli. One of the most common descriptions of optimal experience is that time no longer seems to pass the way it ordinarily does. Hours seem to pass by in minutes, and in general most people report that time seems to pass much faster. With this in mind, Sinatra's intense involvement in singing becomes easier to understand. He found it so satisfying that he actually couldn't do enough of it. No one recorded nearly as much as he did and that was up to the end of his life.

In creative activities, where goals may not be clearly set in advance, a person must develop a strong personal sense of what he intends to do. The artist might not have a visual image of what the finished painting should look like, but when the picture has progressed to a certain point, he should know whether this is what he wanted to achieve or not. And a singer who enjoys singing must have internalized criteria for "good" or "bad," so that after each recording he can say, "Yes, this works; no, this doesn't." Without such internal guidelines, it is impossible to experience flow.

*His Legacy*

## Comparisons with Other Singers

It would be interesting to compare and contrast the similarities and differences in the careers of other singers who overlapped with Sinatra, for example, Dick Haymes, Eddie Fisher, and Tony Bennett. Each singer had an initial big hit and was promoted by major figures in their lives.

In 1950, Eddie Fisher became the hottest act in show business. He was performing before sold-out audiences in the best clubs in the country. His recording of "Thinking of You" broke into *Billboard's* Top 50 list. It was the first of twenty-two consecutive hit records. By the end of 1950 he had been named America's Most Promising New Male Vocalist in *Billboard's* annual disc-jockey poll, as well as Discovery of the Year and Male Singer of the Year. He was called the Jewish Sinatra. By 1954 he had become the most popular singer in America.

Fisher recalls that one afternoon at NBC, "the elevators opened and a group of teenagers piled out and ran right past Sinatra to get to him; they practically pushed him out of their way. By then Sinatra was passé. Sinatra recorded the song "I'm Walking Behind You" and it bombed, then three months later Vic Damone recorded it and again it bombed; Fisher then said, "I recorded it and it was sent right to number one and became my biggest hit." (Fisher, 1999). Between 1950 and 1956 he had twenty-four number 1 hits and nearly fifty songs in the Top 40. However, he suffered badly over his very public and messy divorce from Debbie Reynolds, whom he had married in 1955 and then left for Elizabeth Taylor.

His pulsing delivery and boyish looks made him a lethal heart throb for a generation of teenage girls. Then his marriage to Ms. Taylor fell apart when she took up with Richard Burton.

Fisher writes about how success had come so easily for him and that while in the beginning music mattered more than anything else, soon afterward drugs entered the scene and took over his life. "Maybe it was drugs first and then romance; maybe romance came first. But eventually the music simply became a means to the drugs and the women. I had it all once. And I let it get away. But oh, the women were wonderful." (Fisher, 1999).

When Eddie got his radio and TV shows, he had a man facing him, mouthing the words to every song he sang, leading him on the righteous path to correct time. It didn't hurt him one bit. He went on to become a major singing star.

Seeking to capitalize on the golden Fisher-Reynolds marriage, RKO paired the couple in the musical-comedy film, *Bundle of Joy* (1956) and then cast him with Ms. Taylor in *Butterfield 8* (1960), in a dramatic role that convinced him and the rest of the world that acting was not his destiny.

Later, he entered a long slide and filed for bankruptcy in 1970. His career problems were aggravated by addictions to drugs and gambling, which he wrote about frankly in his first memoir, and its successor, *Been There, Done That"* (1999). He died from complications of hip surgery in 2010. So unfortunately, Fisher did not treat his music with the same seriousness or consideration that Sinatra did. It did not inspire him nor did he find it as rewarding, and then his creativity went nowhere, or as he said the singing wasn't the ballgame, but rather a path to meet women and buy drugs.

Dick Haymes was a popular singer in the Big Band era of World War II. He appeared in more than 30 movies, with major roles in such films as *One Touch of Venus,* with Ava Gardner; *Diamond Horseshoe*, with Betty Grable, and *State Fair*, with Jeanne Crain. It was estimated that Haymes had spent from $1 million to $4 million by the 1950's. His voice was identifiable by its creamy quality, and he often sang nostalgic songs that evoked triumphant yesterdays.

Haymes went through six marriages, each ending in divorce. Like many other stars, he was besieged in his career by prolonged bouts of alcoholism and legal entanglements, which included bankruptcy, income tax problems, alimony claims, and an unsuccessful Federal attempt to deport him to his native Argentina.

At the time of his deportation order, Miss Rita Hayworth, his fourth wife, said, "I'll stick by him to the end." A month after the court victory in 1955, she left him after two years of marriage. He died in 1980 at the age of 61.

Money problems, wife problems, and deportation problems laid Haymes low, and he never quite recovered from these setbacks. While he worked, playing various clubs and appearing occasionally on TV, his career stalled. And, to add to his woes, he developed a serious drinking problem. At the end of his life he was in constant financial difficulties.

If we look at the lives of both Fisher and Haymes, we can discern some psychological underpinnings in the form of destructive behavior once they achieved fame. Fear of success is a widely discussed topic, and it highlights issues of guilt that plague the person who wins in life. In fact, the same can be said about Elvis Presley or the other genius of country music, Hank Williams. I bring this up to highlight the fact that, in contrast, for Sinatra, success was not a deterrent; in fact, he thrived on it.

Of all the singers I have mentioned, only Tony Bennett is still alive. He became an early success with "Because of You" and "Cold Cold Heart." In 1962, Bennett found and recorded "I Left My Heart in San Francisco" and was forevermore part of the Golden Circle of hit-makers. He picks his songs very carefully and many of them are obscure but highly listenable. His coterie of musicians are expert professionals; the backgrounds for his singing, especially in the hands of the redoubtable Ralph Sharon, who died recently, gave him a platform upon which to shine vocally. In addition, Bennett is a fine painter and has had a number of prominent shows.

Tony Bennett followed a very mature and creative path, as his musical career indicates, though he never attained the prominence that Sinatra had in the world. Nor was this was a drive of his, and unless there is a motive for great success, it will never be sought after.

Talent is a large part of accomplishing our dreams. Each of these singers felt at an early age that they wanted to spend their lives as singers. But talent is only a piece of this image of oneself; many are born with musical talent, but only when the talent serves the fuller image and is supported by one's character do we recognize the exceptional. Many may have the talent but few have the ambition that can realize that talent. Ambition is the mystery, and it is individual.

What determines prominence or distinction is the issue of desire, that inability to be other than what you are meant to be. Each of these singers could have lived lives like our own, not in the heights of celebrity, but leading regular lives, and yet they were singled out. Show business best shows this process to us: the quiet revelation of desire, not simply the pronounced motivation to excel in show business, but the character with which these singers acted upon their early desires to sing.

Character is not only what you do, it's the way you do it. Each singer may be different, but certainly some are more memorable and unique. So in this sense "character is fate." In a similar vein, we may ask why some are great and others less so? Why do many singers enter into a mediocre, middle category? For these reasons, success takes on such exaggerated importance because it offers the only way to pole-vault yourself out of the middle category. We are not sure whether Fisher's and Haymes' success fizzled because of a lack of talent or a distorted and troubled personality.

Character refers to deep structures of personality that are particularly resistant to change. Initially, *character* meant a marking instrument that cuts indelible lines and leaves traces. And *style* comes from *stilus* (Latin), a sharp instrument for incising characters (for instance, letters). No wonder style reveals character and is so hard to change. And while the singers I pointed out have a host of differences in their styles and temperament, there are similarities that are important to point out.

Each had a gift of undiluted energy. Once they caught on with the public, they became extremely dedicated to their craft. And for each, once the public came to appreciate their talent, they recorded one record after another. (The list of songs: Bennett, "Boulevard of Broken Dreams"; Fisher, "Anytime"; Haymes, "Little White Lies"; and of course Sinatra, "I'll Never Smile Again".) One crucial common denominator shared by these four is the pure persuasive power of belief in themselves. Determination, high ideals, long hours of work, their values and practices, their tastes and associates, saw to it that their success spiked early in their careers. In each of them was the invincibility of belief in themselves, and in a way each saw himself as attaining an élite status in the world of show business. They become our heroes, the ones who perform inspired deeds for the glory of the populace. These four are exceptional because each was faithful to his personal calling and exemplified his particular determination. Their images – their strivings, their ambitions and their risks – become our instructors. But for Fisher and Haymes, this belief in themselves and their determination could not be sustained; or, as we said before, could it be that success undermined their talent?

## His Superior Attitude

These personifications of heightened imagination burn right into our souls and are its teachers – not only the hero and hero-worship, but tragic figures too, beauties and comics, singers and entertainers. The stagy exaggeration of character traits displayed by extraordinary people belongs to the Romantic tradition.

If the exceptional is the more comprehensive category, then we may comprehend more by studying an extraordinary person—about the depths of human nature and about ourselves. Their songs, their interpretations, tell us so much about human despair, loneliness, failed love, or upbeat enthusiasm. Each of these singers took their music down different roads: Fisher and Haymes were more nostalgic, while Bennett tends to be more lyrical, and of course Sinatra was a blend of all of these, which makes him the superb portrayer of a wide array of emotions.

To change how we see things sometimes takes a kind of falling in love. Like love, a shift of sight can be liberating. You get something back from what you had misperceived as merely worthless. The offensive doldrums of everyday life can be re-evaluated and their usefulness reclaimed. Each of these singers had to deal with his own vision of grandeur and with the restlessness of the heart, its impatience, its dissatisfaction, its yearning. Each wanted to be seen, witnessed, accorded recognition, particularly by their devoted audience. Though everyone at one time or another feels the press of determination to realize his goals in life, it is in the magnified life of celebrities that these demands are most apparent and best documented.

Singers are not merely entertainers. Their role is a far more powerful one. People identify with them in a much more serious and intense way. They exemplify something of a deep meaning – sometimes the hope, loss and the frustrations of love. Great passions are invested in them. They are no longer treated as ordinary humans or even as mere celebrities. Their exploits and failures have great power to exult or to depress.

When their fans talk about these vocalists' performances, it is almost as though they are talking about a secret part of themselves, as if the stars had some secret bonding with them like a message from the angels above.

Thus, Sinatra, Haymes, Fisher and Bennett, in their exploits in the fifties, were not simply a curiosity. They touched something vulnerable in the hearts of millions. They seemed to acquire some form of magic, some miraculous power, some beautiful achievement akin to the deeds of dreams. They also expressed the wish of all who grow old that they might retain their powers down through the years, against the harsh weathering of time. Some truth about life, some deep vein of ancient emotion and human imagination, is the chord that their performances happened to strike.

Their appearance on stage caused enormous excitement, and their bodies were inwardly suffused with a power not their own. For the audience, their beauty spoke for themselves; their excellence pleased; something true shown out. We get so close to them and their songs, so enmeshed in them that we overlook the wonder that they exude.

The old question that arises is: why are some great and others less so? Why the minor leaguer who never makes it to the majors, the middle manager who never gets the corner office with the wide windows, or the fine actor who can't break into a prominent role? In Shakespeare's words from *King Lear*: "It is the stars/the stars above us, govern our conditions." The ancient philosopher, Heraclitus, would counter that and affirm: "It's not the stars; it's your character." However, Shakespeare gives credence to this also when he says in *Julius Caesar*: "The fault, dear Brutus, is not in our stars/But in ourselves."

We might ask why Sinatra was different from the two others and much more grand than Bennett. I think the answer lies in his ambition, which is inherently totalizing, moving forward through taking in more, striving to have, to do and to be more. Sinatra, the ambitious performer, thus stands as a figure who enables us to appreciate life and grasp past, present, and future in a significant shape. Once Sinatra got the bug for singing and performing, nothing stood in his way; he was going to rise to the top no matter what, even if it involved socializing with gangsters, the ones who owned the casinos. And he had a rather remarkable facility for ingratiating himself with important people. So he could just as easily spend an evening with Sam Giancana as with Jack Kennedy—he took over as Master of Ceremonies for Kennedy's inaugural fund raiser.

We see in Sinatra a drive to succeed and to be the best in his field, as was also true of Williams and Jordan. In comparing him to other singers, it all may come down to his inordinate need for success and power. Throughout Sinatra's life, it was all about power.

> "In his art, he perfected the power of captivating a nightclub audience to the point of utter silence, or inducing near-breathlessness in a movie audience as he underwent withdrawal in *The Man with the Golden Arm*. In his personal life, his power need could manifest itself in the ability to seduce a seemingly unattainable woman – Ava Gardner. Sinatra fed off this power because it seemed to provide the legitimacy he so strongly desired." (Santopiero, p. 78)

The power motive, as mentioned in the last chapter, was a dominating force throughout his life. Power has to do with having an impact, control or influence over another person, group, or the world at large. Certainly, individuals with high power needs would be more competitive and aggressive. Men with high power needs are more apt to fight, drink, gamble, and attempt to exploit women sexually, and we can see this motive as a dominating force in Sinatra's experience. (McClelland, 1985).

Throughout his life, Sinatra came to live in a world he had created himself, created in part to control it. This strong power need can be defined as *having impact*. One way to have impact is by strong action, such as by assault and aggression. We know this from the incident of his punching Lee Mortimer because Mortimer had insulted him.

Another part of the power motive is to give help, assistance or advice. If you help someone, it looks as if you are trying to save them, which of course you are. For help to be given, help must be received. And in accepting a gift, or help, the receiver can be perceived as acknowledging that he is weaker, at least in this respect, than the person who is giving him help. Thus, giving and receiving may have a "zero sum" quality analogous to winning or losing. To the extent that one person wins or gives, the other must lose or receive. This in no way would cancel Sinatra's compassion for another person, though it speaks to another side of his motivation.

Tina Sinatra described her father as a man who deeply needed love but who couldn't connect emotionally with other people. Perhaps this explains the power dynamic many people observed between Frank and his friends: he demanded total loyalty and rejected friends and moved them completely out of his life when he felt betrayed. As one of his songs says, it's a matter of "all or nothing at all." When a friend was hurt, sick, or down and out, Frank was at the friend's side loyally and consistently; but if Frank perceived that a friend even mildly breached his trust, that friend could be threatened, screamed at, and cut off completely. Many people who knew Frank well echoed the sentiment that Frank could be the most generous person in the world or the most selfish and cruel, depending on the circumstances.

His concern for his reputation, and how he believed others looked up to him and viewed him, was always on his mind. He was continually concerned about his prestige and his appearance to others. Another finding by McClelland (1975) is that feeling powerful can be related to drinking more alcohol, that alcohol makes the individual feel strong and vigorous. Frank's drinking likely contributed to his violent outbursts. Friends reported that when Frank was bored and liquored up, he would go out looking for fights. Those who knew Frank well knew to get out of the way when he had had too much to drink. By the 1960's, Frank's drinking had become a disturbingly entrenched part of his life. Frank joked about his alcohol use, but some friends claim that Frank could drink an entire bottle of Jack Daniels in one sitting, and remembered that while Frank rarely appeared inebriated in public, in private he frequently showed signs of extreme drunkenness.

There are so many instances that highlight Frank's power needs. Zsa Zsa Gabor claimed that Frank had pushed his way into her house and refused to leave until she had sex with him, which she eventually did, so that he would leave before her daughter woke up. And a similar claim was made by Marlene Dietrich, who said that Frank would not leave her house until she went to bed with him. And similar experiences were voiced by others, including an aspiring actress named Sandra Giles, who stated that Frank acted as though he thought he was a god and could do anything that he wanted with impunity. This was all in the name of feelings of power. And yet because of these power needs, Frank could also attain the status of a mighty entertainment warrior, so we see that the need for power can operate in many different directions with positive and negative features.

The man who is high in power needs tends to accumulate whatever signs or symbols give him prestige in the group in which he belongs. So Sinatra had three expensive homes, and when in Vegas he stayed at the Sands.

Another interesting aspect of Sinatra's life was his need to associate and become friends with the most powerful people. Sinatra was invited to the White House both by Nixon and Reagan. In fact, he was so often invited to the White House with Nancy Reagan that gossip soon emerged about a possible relationship between the two of them. But we can assume what it must have felt like having this open invitation to enter the sacred home of the President.

When we think back and try to understand the underpinnings of Sinatra's life, we come to the realization that he was driven by an invincibility of belief. Though at times he could be found morally reprehensible, his belief allowed him to go forward uncorrupted in the midst of some dirty doings. There is something in his actions that meshes well with the American character and that accounts for why he is such an eminent representative of its style.

Frank's need to associate with strong political figures goes back to 1944. Franklin Roosevelt was running for re-election and Frank became actively involved in the campaign. Working with the Democratic Party, he appeared at fundraisers, spoke at Carnegie Hall, and appeared on broadcasts in support of Roosevelt. Frank was invited to, and attended, an afternoon reception at the White House during this time, even though it earned FDR some negative press for wasting his time with a "crooner." He appeared with FDR's running mate, Harry Truman, at a huge event in Madison Square Garden the week before the election, and attended two to three campaign events a day immediately prior to the election.

At the other end of this spectrum was his need to cultivate very powerful gangsters such as Giancana. It appeared as if by associating with these gangsters he was able to feel even more powerful. His power needs far outdistanced those of other crooners.

In 1960, when JFK's father, Joe Kennedy, who had imported liquor during Prohibition, decided to help his son run for the Presidency, he sold his interest in that business and turned his powerful will to getting JFK elected. For help in this pursuit, Joe Kennedy turned to Frank Sinatra. Frank, as Joe knew, was connected to mobster Sam Giancana, head of the Chicago mob that Joe needed on his side to get the vote for his son in the swing states of Illinois and West Virginia. Sinatra agreed to talk to Giancana and see what could be done. With Frank's help, JFK won the primary elections in West Virginia and Chicago. Voters were alternately bribed or threatened into voting for JFK. In return, Joe Kennedy promised Giancana and other mobsters that their reward for help with the election would be that his son's administration would relax law enforcement in regard to Mafia activity.

Sinatra was ecstatic over his association with JFK and he couldn't do enough to further his election. In addition, he threw parties with multitudes of beautiful actresses and hired prostitutes to satisfy JFK's sexual appetite. Frank also took the additional step of setting him up with Judith Campbell. Evidence points to the likelihood that Judith was a high-end prostitute for the Mob and was given as a gift to JFK. Judith was introduced to JFK at the Sands and continued a sexual relationship with him that lasted into his Presidency.

Frank then launched into a very active role in the election and devised two songs with different lyrics, "High Hopes" and "All the Way," which became the anthems of JFK's campaign. He brought the Rat Pack and other famous entertainers into the work of campaigning for JFK. In addition to having the politician appear at the Sands, Frank arranged for Sammy Davis Jr., Nat King Cole, Ella Fitzgerald, and others to perform at rallies for JFK. Davis postponed his wedding to a white woman until after the election for the purpose of avoiding the negative publicity that it would bring to JFK. Frank and the others raised huge sums of money for JFK's campaign.

Later, Ronald Reagan asked Frank to direct his inaugural gala. Telling the papers that he simply hoped the things he was hearing about Frank weren't true, he continued to welcome Frank into the White House. The gala raised millions of dollars. Shortly thereafter, Frank applied for a new gambling license from the Nevada gambling authority. He put down Reagan's name as a reference, and Reagan told the board that Frank was honest and loyal. Frank was granted the license despite being unable to explain various associations with mobsters. It was interesting to see how much Reagan was impressed with Sinatra and wanted his friendship.

Reagan asked him to organize his second inaugural gala, and, in 1985, he awarded Frank the Medal of Freedom, the highest award available to a civilian, for his humanitarian and civil rights work.

## Myth of Success

The belief in America that all men and women living in accordance with certain rules can make of their lives what they will, exclusively through their own efforts, has been widely popular for well over a century. The cluster of ideas surrounding this conviction forms the American myth of success.

Many myths born in the nineteenth century have withered and disappeared; the myth of success, however, continues to flourish. Conveyed in a massive amount of literature, it stands as one of the most enduring expressions of American popular ideals. The term "myth" does not imply something entirely false. Rather, it is used to denote a complex of profoundly held attitudes and values that condition the way we view the world and understand our experience. The success myth reflects what millions believe society is or ought to be. The degree to which opportunity has or has not been available in our society is a different question, but the *belief* that opportunity exists for all is widely held

In this sense, Sinatra represents an urge in all of us to do whatever we have to in order to rise to the top. In some ways, everything he touched turned to gold. Yes, there were major setbacks in the early fifties, but he rose above them, emerging even bigger in the eyes of the American public. His talent meshed superbly with a driven quality that brought him to the top of his profession as a performer, businessman, and fellow traveler with the big winners of power and wealth.

In many ways, Sinatra's rise to fame bears a resemblance to Norman Vincent Peale's gospel of "the power of positive thinking." A few figures concerning his popularity may serve as some indication of this kind of inspiration in contemporary America. In 1957, Peale reached an audience estimated at thirty million a week. In 1954, 150 newspapers carried his syndicated column, "Confident Living"; his radio show, *The Art of Living*, was broadcast into a million homes; his television show was shown on over 140 stations; and his magazine *Guideposts* had a circulation of 650,000. His *Power of Positive Thinking* (1952) had sales of two million by 1955 and was only surpassed in the nonfiction best-seller category during these years by the *Revised Standard Version of the Bible*.

Peale addresses himself to the need to build the individual ego. "Every normal person," he writes, "wants power over circumstances; power over situations; power over fear; power over weakness; power over themselves." His main thesis is that people who would achieve success and happiness must think positively. The victorious "train the mind to think victory" and as a result they attain it.

Discussing the meaning of success and the individual's quest for power in our society, psychoanalyst Karen Horney notes, "The striving for power serves in the first place as a protection against helplessness which... is one of the basic elements in anxiety... the weaker he in fact factually becomes, the more anxiously he has to avoid anything that has a faint resemblance to weakness." Furthermore, she observes, "Protection against helplessness and insignificance or humiliation can be had, in our culture, by striving for possession, inasmuch as wealth gives power and prestige."

The point is that while Sinatra is seen as a huge success who courts the most powerful figures in the world, his life impresses us with our own fantasies of power and success, and we can identify with him through his songs. Few other successes in our culture are easy to get close to, but Sinatra remains accessible to us; even the song "My Way," touches us all, as we all have some hope that we can also do it "our" way.

Some writers attempt to tear him down because of the energy and force he mustered to reach the top of the ladder. Yet for many others, this need to muscle his way forward became an inspiration for us all.

When we think about it, the roots of human dissatisfaction and restlessness go as deep into the spirit as any human drive – even deeper than any other drive. Nothing stills the human spirit. Nothing fulfills it. It is not a need like hunger, thirst, or an itch, for such needs are easily satisfied. It is a need enmeshed with sex, yet orgasmic satisfaction does not always quiet it. Most writers refer to it as "desire," passion. Distorted as it was in the case of Eddie Fisher, the drive for perfection can propel an ugly and considerably less than perfect human development. True, straight, and well targeted, it soars like an arrow toward the intrinsic beauty of humanity. The renditions and interpretation of lyrics nourish this drive as well as any other institution in our society. If this drive is often distorted, even its distortions testify to its power, in the same way liars mark out the boundaries of truth.

In our everyday conversations with friends, wives or husbands, we are unprepared to speak about the things we love the most or the things that bother and hurt us. Grown men among us are virtually inarticulate about anything that touches their souls. Women can get little out of the men in their lives, since they speak one language, and men another. The streets of America do not reflect all of us in stories and anecdotes rich with many years of human struggle. But popular singers tutor us in the basic lived experiences of humanist tradition.

Human plans involve ironies. The decisions we make with little attention turn out to be major turning points, and what we prepare for with exquisite detail often never happens. So many of Sinatra's songs make explicit the almost nameless dreads of daily human life: aging, failure, loss or guilt. Sifting through his repertoire, we find these thoughts in every performance.

He is a portrait of an individual with great smoldering forces of human desire and frustration and discontent, something we all have in us too, part of mankind as a whole. And because, with all his strength, he's still up against something he can't seem to understand, there's an ironic perspective too. He then reflects about part of our own lives. Much of his singing is a story of the loss and regain of identity.

When critics talk of the richness of his voice, how his voice enthralls and creates distinctive moods as well as giving rise to intense moods, they may be referring to its intricacies and depth. This is the way a talented actor portrays a part; the actor is able to imbue the characters with a deepness and power. Sinatra is able to do this through his singing. When you listen to some songs that were sung again and again over periods of years, you realize they are not always sung the same way, as a different understanding has evolved with age.

His audiences have their favorites: some like the smooth, tender crooner of "I'll Never Smile Again" with Tommy Dorsey; for others, he's the bruised, tough, but vulnerable romantic of "In the Wee Small Hours of the Morning." Others prefer the ultimate swaggering playboy of "Come Fly With Me." And then there are many others for whom Sinatra is the persevering hero of anthems like "My Way," "A Very Good Year," and of course, "New York, New York."

That he was able to change styles as he aged points to his talent as an actor and his willingness to explore and evolve into different characters. And in these performances and recordings he discovered a new relationship to the audience which was so close, so intimate, that it broke down the wall which so often separates an artist from his audience.

The prerequisite for this ability to some extent rests on his talent. Talent is an amalgam of high sensitivity, easy vulnerability, high sensory equipment (seeing, hearing, touching, tasting intensely); the desire to communicate one's own experience and sensations, and make oneself heard and seen. It is also necessary for one to have a point of view about the surrounding world, the society in which we live, and a point of view as to how art can reflect judgment.

## Deliberate Practice

There is a term in psychology called "deliberate practice." First introduced in a 1993 *Psychological Review* article, the notion of deliberate practice went far beyond the simple idea of hard work. It really conveyed a method of continual skill improvement, which does not involve a mere execution or repetition of already attained skills, but rather repeated attempts to *reach beyond one's current level*. Aspiring performers therefore concentrate on improving specific aspects of their work by engaging in practice activities designed to change and refine particular mechanisms, requiring successive refinement and feedback. This could be seen as a kind of practice that doesn't take "no" for an answer; practice that perseveres; the type of practice in which the individual keeps raising the bar on what he or she considers success.

Deliberate practice requires a constant self-critique, an intense restlessness, a passion to aim consistently just beyond one's capability so that daily disappointment and failure are actually desired, along with a never-ending resolve to dust oneself off and try again and again. It also requires enormous life-altering amounts of time – a daily, grinding, commitment to becoming better. In the long run, the results produce success; however, in the short term, from day to day and month to month, there's nothing particularly enjoyable about the process or the substantial sacrifices involved. Certainly there is a difference between leisure players, who tend to enjoy themselves casually much of the time, and dedicated achievers who become glued to the gritty process of getting better.

The non-achievers seem to be missing something in their process- one or more aspects of style or intensity of practice, or technique, or mindset, or response to failure. Becoming great at something requires the right combination of resources, mentality, strategies, persistence, and time; these may be tools that are available to everyone, but the real gift comes from one's mindset, the willingness to invest enormous time and effort at self-improvement.

In order to be very successful or exceptional, as one matures, one needs to be increasingly active in personal development. An individual has to develop hunger, be open to career advice, and hone his social skills or his intriguing persona. This could be a summary of Sinatra's professional life, that he constantly improved over the years because he had to, he was driven to, and he could not stay the same. This need to continually get better and better seemed to be embedded in his character.

## DISCIPLINE

Every serious singer must demand total discipline of himself if he or she really means to be successful. Sinatra won with a thorough, backbreaking discipline in his work, in his examination of his materials and his relationship to them, and in his dedication. There are singers who tend to continually deliver a song the same way as they did before, which means they are not truly using themselves. They are simply playing the same few notes in themselves over and over again, without a real search for. or need to inject, innovation and freshness. Often, after an initial success, these kinds of singers simply copy from themselves, imitating moments and effects which have worked for them before. They rely on a quality which they feel has succeeded with an audience, and end up singing the same material in a tiresome and repetitive manner. What established Sinatra's uniqueness is that he was always fresh, inventive, and exciting.

We might say that Sinatra both echoed and lived the life that Vince Lombardi, the successful coach of the Green Bay Packers football team, described. Lombardi said, "The quality of any man's life has got to be a full measure of that man's personal commitment to excellence and to victory regardless of what field he may be in."

The statement "Winning is the only thing" becomes controversial for many people who feel that there is too much emphasis on winning at all costs. However, Coach Lombardi reminded us many times that there is no laughter in losing. He went on to say that the reality is that human beings are competitive, and the most competitive games draw the most competitive people. They know the rules and the objectives when they get in the game. The objective is to win, fairly, squarely, decently, by the rules – but to win. These remarks resound in Sinatra's life, since he exemplifies another of Lombardi's statements: "I don't care what people say about me as long as I win. That's what I get paid for." And also, "All the glamour, all of the noise, all of the excitement, all of the color, they linger only in the memory, but the spirit, the will to excel, the will to win, they go on forever." (Lombardi )

*His Legacy*

## THE EARLY YEARS

The big band crooner Sinatra, who learned some of his smooth, *legato* phrasing from watching Tommy Dorsey's breathing while playing trombone, can be heard developing his early style on the discs he recorded with Dorsey. Sinatra would never again be as tenderly, achingly romantic, or as pure of voice, as he was in his first decade as a solo singer with the lush arrangements of Axel Stordahl. These recordings can be heard from the Columbia years, 1943 to 1952.

## THE MIDDLE YEARS

Sinatra's work with Capitol Records in the mid-to-late 1950's marks the most significant change in his voice and style. He called himself a saloon singer, abandoning most of the smooth, sweet tone of the Columbia years for a more masculine, dynamic sound, where he was either a swaggering swinger or a tough-but-tender sensitive guy in charge, depending on the tune, mood and tempo.

During these years, Sinatra perfected the heartbeat rhythm, which is just what it implies, a tempo neither swing-fast nor ballad-slow, of a persona who made every song a story. It was during these years that he developed the "concept" albums. Of those, *In the Wee Small Hours* and *Only the Lonely* were instrumental in developing the idea of the American Popular Songbook "standard," with arrangements by Nelson Riddle, who did more than anyone else to create Sinatra's signature middle-years sound. *Come Fly With Me* is the singer's most consistently swinging album, courtesy of arranger Billy May.

## THE LATER YEARS

The saloon singer became a concert singer in his later years, especially the 1970's and early '80's, when he was at his mature concert peak. Songs became more than stories, they became grand epics ("Solioquy") or anthems ("My Way"). With his own Reprise label, Sinatra also pursued Top 40 ambitions and some of those can be heard on the representative four-disc album, *The Reprise Collection*.

But the most representative later-years album is *The Concert Sinatra* (Reprise), which finds him in excellent voice, singing what were obviously his favorite songs, since he returned to them again and again in concert—and never more definitively than here.

The close friendship Steve and Eydie enjoyed with Sinatra during his last years gave Lawrence a reason to reflect on Nelson's work with Sinatra:

> Riddle expanded Frank's musical horizons. As great and as innovative as Frank was musically and as an interpreter lyrically, Nelson gave him a sound that up until that point he didn't have as musically as that. From then on, it gave him an identification that they both really wallowed in—the straight quarter notes tied to each other became the driving force. He really overpowered Frank, lifted him up to that climax, threw him over the top, and then brought him back to where they wanted to settle. There are only a handful of people that you can think of who understood each other so well. Both of them became bigger because of each other.

Ray Connolly of the *Sunday Times* wrote: "Sinatra has become the keeper of the flame for everyone 40 to 80. His songs distill the youth, the nostalgia of millions. He also happens to be the best at it; an artist of colossal stature. He swings, he speaks, he shapes songs like no one else. That's genius."

He never burned out, and the fact he kept going is, to his audience, a reaffirmation of themselves. Sinatra is magic to those who came of age in the 1940's. His art, the unmatched phrasing and breath control, the emotional readings of American popular songs, the work with the finest arrangers, conductors, and musicians in the country, the untiring musical perfectionism, has left an indelible mark on the American Song Book, "What makes Sinatra so marvelous this late in life in his unflagging commitment to his craft and art. He never gave up, never let even the silliest material overcome his sense of style, never (for long, at least) allowed the routine of performance or the indulgences of vast wealth to dull his desire to do the very best he could." (Rockwell, 1985)

So in the end, what can we learn from looking at Sinatra's life? What has he left for us to see that would make our lives more rounded, more exciting, and more fulfilled? What monumental present has he bestowed upon us? A man who has made such a mark in this world must leave some wisdom, some truths that will lead to our happiness. I think the truths he has left would go like this:

- Find what you love to do and invest yourself in it.
- Plan your goals carefully and don't underestimate your talents.
- Learn to be expressive and make an impact on the world around you.
- Keep the energy level going as intensely as you can.
- Develop a circle of friends and play off them.
- Treat yourself like a king or queen and others will then treat you in a similar manner.
- Get as emotional as you are able.
- Stay close to the excitement of adolescence.
- Be as generous as you can and you will win the love of your friends.
- And above all, keep listening to the records of Sinatra.

Steve Ross, who was the chairman of Time Warner, made this telling remark about success: "Think like a winner. Act like a winner. Hang out with winners."

When you put this template over the life of Sinatra, you have the essence of a winner—a man who tried to get as much out of life as he could, who never stopped making an impact on his world, and yet throughout, was always his own person, because he did it His Way.

## CONCLUSION

Frank Sinatra occupies a unique place in the history of American popular culture. On stage, on screen, and of course behind a microphone, Sinatra was a sensational artist. His life, both public and private, was an amazing sequence of contradictions – he was tough and tender, a lover and a fighter, a star and a loner. Sinatra was our most glorified champion and headstrong underdog—both the Comeback Kid and the Chairman of the Board. Yet, through it all his was always The Voice: the voice that has touched millions and held them captive in its trance; the voice of a legend.

He is the most imitated, most listened to, most recognized voice of the second half of the twentieth century. His tape-recorded voice was heard by the Apollo 12 astronauts as they orbited the moon, and his 206 CDs currently in print make him the most comprehensively digitally preserved music-maker in the history of recorded sound. The story of Sinatra is the story of a kid from Hoboken who achieved one of the most powerful positions in American culture and became a friend of a multitude of celebrities, Presidents, and high-ranking members of the Mafia.

The greatest pop singer in the history of America, he evolved from a pleasant lightweight performer on film to the most versatile male presence in movies. In fact, no other actor in Hollywood history has ever ranged so widely and so believably over such a long period of time. Through sheer force of talent and willpower, Sinatra fulfilled his dream of movie stardom, won Hollywood's top honors, and emerged as a top-flight dramatic actor.

So we have a person who has conquered the highest realms of entertainment in both singing and acting. In viewing Sinatra's life, we are witnessing the power of character and ambition and the extraordinary factor of fate – how it arrives and shows itself, what it demands, its side effects, and how it excites us and gives our lives an imaginary dimension. His life had much to do with his feelings of uniqueness, of grandeur, and the restlessness of the heart—its impatience, its dissatisfaction, its yearning. He knew that he was blessed with one of the most exceptional voices and a keen acting ability, and he was not going to stand by and watch his talent evolve slowly. No, his life was one of action, quickness, versatility – for him, there wasn't a moment to waste. He nurtured his talent and continued to grow as an artist, always inventing new parts of himself. His life could serve as an inspiration for all of us, in that it represents the old adage, "there isn't a moment to waste" if you want to be a success. Or in the words of Vince Lombardi, "Success rests not only on ability, but upon commitment, loyalty and pride. The will to excel and the will to win, they endure. They are more important than any events that occasion them." I believe that this is the lesson that Sinatra has left us. And it's a great lesson that speaks of endurance, commitment to excellence, belief in oneself, and the will to succeed.

# BIBLIOGRAPHY

Aristotle, *Poetics*, trans. Ingram Bywater, in *Introduction to Aristotle*, ed. Richard McKeon (2nd ed.; Chicago: Univ. of Chicago Press, 1973).

Bacall, L. *By My*self. New York: Alfred A. Knopf. 1979.

Brook, J.A. 1992. *Freud and spitting.* International Review of Psycho-Analyis 19:335-348.

Cahn. S. *I Should Care.* New York. Pyramid Books. 1974.

Csikszentmihalyim, M. *Flow: The Psychology of Optimal Experience.* New York: Harper & Row. 1990.

Clarke, D. (1998). All or nothing at all: A life of Frank Sinatra. New York: Macmillan.

Eissler, K. 1967. Psychopathology and creativity. *American Imago* 24:35-81.

Fleiss, R. 1944. The metapsychogy of the analyst. *Psychoanalytic Quarterly* 13:211-227.

Friedwald, W. *Sinatra! The song is you.* New York: Da Capo Press. 1997.

Jewell, D. *Frank Sinatra. A Celebration.* New York: Applause Books. 1999.

Gartner, J.D. *The Hypomanic Edge.* New York: Simon and Schuster. 2005.

Giddins, G. *Bing Crosby: A Pocketful Of Dreams.* New York: Little, Brown & Co. 2001.

Howelett, J. *Frank Sinatra.* New York: Simon and Schuster. 1979.

Hillman, J. *The Soul's Code.* New York: Warner Books. 1997.

Freud, S. 1923. The ego and the id. *Standard Edition* 19:3-66. London: Hogarth Press, 1961.

_____.1930. Civilization and its discontents. Standard Edition 21:59-145. London: Hogarth Press, 1961.

_____.1940. An outline of psycho-analysis. Standard Edition 23:141- 207. London: Hogarth Press, 1964.

Gedo, M. 1980. *Picasso: Art as Autobiography*. Chicago: University of Chicago Press.

Greenacre, P. 1957. The childhood of the artist. *Psychoanalytic Study of the Child*. 12:47-72. New York: International Universities Press.

_____.1958. The family romance of the artist. Psychoanalytic Study of the Child. 13:9-36.

Giddins, G. (1998). Frank Sinatra: the ultimate in theater. In *Visions of Jazz*. New York: Oxford. 1998.

Halberstram, D. *Playing for Keeps*. New York Broadway Books, 2000.

Hamill, P. Why Sinatra matters. New York: Little, Brown and Company. 1998.

Huffington, A. (2002). Maria Callas: The Woman behind the Legend. New York: Cooper Square, Press.

Jewell, D. *Frank Sinatra. A Celebration*. New York: Applause Books. 1999.

Kakutani, M. Sinatra, The Life, (book review) New York Times, May 17, 2005.

Kaplan, J. Frank. The Voice. New York: Doubleday. 2010.

Kaplan, J. Sinatra, The Chairman. New York: Doubleday. 2015.

Kelley, K. 1986. His way. New York: Bantam Books.

Rose, G.F. 1987. Trauma & mastery in life and art. New Haven; Yale University Press.

Lehman, D. A. A Fine Romance. New York: Schocken Books. 2009.

Levinson, P.J. *Tommy Dorsey*. DaCapo Press. 1995.

Levinson, P.J. (1999). *Trumpet Blues*. The Life of Harry James. New York: Oxford University Press.

Levinson, P.J. *September in the Rain*. The Life of Nelson Riddle. New York: First Taylor Trade Publishing. 2005.

Maehr, M. & Braskamp, L. *The Motivation Factor*. Lexington: D.C. Heath, 1986.

Maccoby, M. *The Gamesman*. New York: Simon & Schuster. 1976.

Maccoby, M. *The Productive Narcissist. New York:* Broadway. 2003.

Novak, M. *The Joy of Sports*. Latham: Madison Books. 1994.

Mustazza, L. ed. *Frank Sinatra and Popular Culture*. Westport: Praeger. 1998.

Petkov, S. & Mustazza, L. eds. The Sinatra Reader. New York: OxfordUniversity Press. 1995.Phillips, A. New York Times. How Much Does Monogamy Tell Us. October 2, 1998

Prigozy, R. The Life of Dick Haymes. Jackson: University Press of Mississippi. 2006.

Rockwell, J. (1985). *Sinatra: An American classic.* (New York: Random House.

Santopietro, T. Sinatra in Hollywood. New York: St. Martins Press. 2008.

Schafer, R. 1982. The analytic attitude. New York: Basic Books.

Schneider, D. E. The Psychoanalyst and the artist. New York: Mentor Book. 1962.

Segal, H. A psychoanalytic approach to aesthetics. In M. Klein et al (eds) New Directions in Psychoanalysis. London: Tavistock Publications. 1955.

Shaw, A. Sinatra, the entertainer. New York, A Delilah Book. 1982.

Sinatra, B. *My Life With Frank*. New York: Three Rivers Press. 2011.

Sinatra, N. (1986). Frank Sinatra, My Father. New York: Coronet Books.

Taraborrelli, J. R. Sinatra: beyond the legend. New York: Birchland Press, 1997.

Torme, M. *My Singing Teachers.* New York: Oxford University Press. 1994.

Vare, E.A (ed.) Frank Sinatra and the American Dream. *Protecting Sinatra Against the Big Beef Story*. Buckley, C. Boulevard Books. 1995.

Weiss, R. The American Myth of Success. New York: Basic Books, 1969.

Zehme, B . *The Way You Wear Your Hat. New York:* HarperCollins. 1997.